UNDERSTANDING NARCISSISM IN CLINICAL PRACTICE

The Society of Analytic Psychology Monograph Series
Hazel Robinson (Series Editor)
Published and distributed by Karnac Books

Other titles in the SAP Monograph Series

Undestanding Perversion in Clinical Practice
Fiona Ross

Orders
Tel: +44 (0)20 8969 4454; Fax: +44 (0)20 8969 5585
Email: shop@karnacbooks.com
www.karnacbooks.com

UNDERSTANDING NARCISSISM IN CLINICAL PRACTICE

*Hazel Robinson
& Victoria Graham Fuller*

KARNAC

LONDON   NEW YORK

First published in 2003 by
H. Karnac (Books) Ltd.
6 Pembroke Buildings, London NW10 6RE

Copyright © 2003 by Hazel Robinson & Victoria Graham Fuller

The rights of Hazel Robinson & Victoria Graham Fuller to be identified as the authors of this work have been asserted in accordance with §§ 77 and 78 of the Copyright Design and Patents Act 1988.

All rights reserved. No part of this publication may be reproduced, stored in a retrieval system, or transmitted, in any form or by any means, electronic, mechanical, photocopying, recording, or otherwise, without the prior written permission of the publisher.

British Library Cataloguing in Publication Data

A C.I.P. for this book is available from the British Library

ISBN 978 1 85575 938 1

Edited, designed, and produced by Cortex Publishing

Printed in Great Britain

www.karnacbooks.com

CONTENTS

About the Authors   vii

Preface to the Series   ix

Introduction   1

CHAPTER ONE
The Story of Narcissus:
a psycho-sexual dynamic   5

CHAPTER TWO
Some Clinical Examples   13
    Alan
    Bridget
    Chandit
    David
    Elisabeth
    Flora
    Gill

CHAPTER THREE
Manifestations of Narcissism   31
   Some manifestations of narcissistic
   disorder in everyday life
   Gender issues
   Assessment for psychotherapy
   Some possible contraindications
   Narcissistic disorders in psychiatry

CHAPTER FOUR
Therapeutic Challenges   43
   Assessment
   Establishing the Therapeutic Alliance
   Negotiating a crisis
   Ongoing work

CHAPTER FIVE
The Development of Narcissism as a
Clinical Concept   67
   Freud
   Jung
   Klein
   Kernberg and Kohut
   Winnicott, Fordham and Bowlby
   Bion, Rosenfeld and Steiner
   Afterword

References   85

Index   93

ABOUT THE AUTHORS

Victoria Graham Fuller is a Jungian analyst in private practice in London, and a former chairman of SAP Council. She has taught and supervised for a number of training institutions as well as the NHS. She has contributed many papers to books and journals, including a chapter in *Supervising and Being Supervised: A Practice in Search of a Theory* (2003, ed. Wiener, Duckham and Mizen, Palgrave). She is also centrally involved in training for The Institute of Group Analysis where she is a qualified member.

Hazel Robinson is a Jungian analyst. She qualified with the Guild of Psychotherapists and the Society of Analytical Psychology, and has worked in private practice in London since 1985. Coming from a background in psychiatric social work, she has continued to practice part-time in the public sector, with children and families, and, latterly, within adult mental health. She has taught on several counselling and psychotherapy courses and has lectured on aspects of psychotherapy in psychiatric settings. She is the originator and editor of this series.

PREFACE TO THE SERIES

This series of clinical practice monographs is being produced primarily for the benefit of trainees on psychotherapy and psychodynamic counselling courses. The authors are Jungian analysts who have trained at the Society of Analytical Psychology, with extensive experience of teaching both theory and practice.

The rationale for this series is in part to do with the expensive and time-consuming task of accessing all the pertinent books and papers for any one clinical subject. These single-issue monographs have been kept relatively brief and cannot claim to be comprehensive, but we hope that each volume brings together some of the major theorists and their ideas in a comprehensible way, including references to significant and interesting texts.

Much of the literature provided for students of psychotherapy has been generated from four or five-times weekly analytic work, which can be confusing for students whose psychodynamic courses may be structured on the basis of less frequent sessions. The authors of these monographs have aimed to hold this difference in mind. A decision was taken to maintain the terms 'therapist' and 'patient' throughout, although the clinical work referred to ranges from once weekly to five-times weekly. We have also borrowed shamelessly from the work of our supervisees in many settings, for which we thank them. We are even more indebted to our patients. Where a patient's material is recognisable, their permission to publish has been given. In other cases, we have amalgamated and disguised clinical material to preserve anonymity.

When a training is 'eclectic', that is, offering several different psychodynamic perspectives, a particular difficulty can arise with the integration – or rather *non-integration* of psychoanalytic and Jungian analytic ideas. The teaching on such trainings is often presented in blocks: a term devoted to 'Freud', another to 'Jung' and so on. It is frequently the students who are left with the job of trying to see where these do and do not fit together, and this can be a daunting, even depressing experience. SAP analysts are in a better position than most to offer some help here, because its members have been working on this integration since the organisation was founded in 1946. Although retaining a strong relationship with 'Zurich' or 'Classical' Jungian scholarship, SAP members have evolved equally strong links with psychoanalysis. Recent years have brought a number of joint conferences to supplement the many individual 'cross-party' alliances.

Any patient, but particularly a trainee, will naturally tend to adopt the language of his or her therapist when talking about their work. Those readers who are unfamiliar with Jungian terms may wish to consult the *Critical Dictionary of Jungian Analysis* (Samuels, Plaut & Shorter, 1986), whilst those unfamiliar with psychoanalytic terms may turn to *The Language of Psychoanalysis* (Laplanche & Pontalis, 1988). Strangely though, all patients are united by their human suffering far more than they are divided by language. Just as people from non-Western cultures have to make what they can of their western-trained psychotherapists, so each patient-therapist pair eventually evolve a unique way of understanding their joint experiences in the consulting-room. It is our view that each stream of psychotherapy has strengths and weaknesses, and the wise trainee will take the best bits from each. We hope that this series may help a little with the psychodynamic 'Tower of Babel'.

We want to thank Karnac Books for their patience and help in bringing the series to publication. Our intention is to add to the series of monographs each year, gradually building up a 'stable' of texts on the principle clinical issues. I therefore want to end by thanking my colleagues within the SAP for their work so far – and for their work to come.

Hazel Robinson
Series Editor

INTRODUCTION

"In the voluminous literature on narcissism, there are probably only two facts on which everyone agrees: first, that the concept is one of the most important contributions of psychoanalysis; second, that is it one of the most confusing..."
Pulver, 1986, p. 91

In the years since Freud's first contribution to the subject, narcissism as a clinical construct has stimulated enormous clinical and theoretical interest in the field of psychotherapy, giving rise to a mass of theories and clinical data. Narcissism has been viewed as a fixation on self-love, a special type of object relations, an attempt to regulate fluctuations in self-esteem, a particular way of relating to others, a failure to work through a developmental phase, to name just a few. This book explores the clinical condition of narcissistic disorder in various ways, attempting to cover some of the many psychoanalytic concepts associated with it.

Modern western attitudes to 'self-help' and 'self-realisation' represent a 'healthy' form of narcissism, but there comes a point when the emphasis on individual ideals can damage or destroy loving relationships with others. This can be looked at, in part, as a cultural phenomenon. In the

1970's Christopher Lasch observed how competitive individualism in the United Sates, taken to extremes, evolved over decades into a 'culture of narcissism' (1979).

The subtle perversion of healthy narcissistic aims is captured by the pejorative use of the adjective 'narcissistic' in western literature and media to describe someone who is behaving in a self-centred or self-important way. It sums up the common experience of a person who has been taken over by internal pressure to perform well, to 'look good', at any cost. This may be temporary, often arising in reaction to stressful events such as interviews, but when narcissistic traits are rigidly established, and cause severe impairment in psychological and everyday functioning, they can be said to constitute a disorder. People suffering from this disorder have insufficient ego-strength or resilience to recover from everyday problems, and cannot sustain their psychic equilibrium without splitting, dissociation, and constant efforts to gain admiration and reassurance.

Stories and myths often express mans' attempts to represent psychic conflicts. Western literature provides many examples of characters caught up in the difficulties resulting from pathological narcissism, for example *Anna Karenina* (Tolstoy) and *Portrait of a Lady* (James). Films such as Ingmar Bergman's *Persona* (1966), *How to Marry a Millionaire* (Negulesco, 1953) and *American Beauty* (Mendes, 2000) also depict such dilemmas (see Berman, 1990 and Dougherty, 2001).

The term narcissism originates from Ovid's myth which is presented and discussed in Chapter 1. Although there were many who admired the beautiful boy, Narcissus, he rejected them all. His relationship – or rather, *non-relationship*, with the nymph Echo, who could not initiate speech, illustrates the intra-psychic dynamic within which a narcissistically damaged patient is caught. Both figures are isolated behind impenetrable barriers to relationship. When Narcissus *did* fall in love - with his own, unattainable, reflection, he became conscious of his predicament, and killed himself.

How might 'Narcissus' and 'Echo' appear in the consulting-room? In Chapter 2 we offer a series of brief clinical examples. Manifestations of narcissistic disorder across the spectrum are clarified in Chapter 3. Freud's original (1914) description of narcissism is a recognisable feature of *narcissistic personality disorder*. The treatment of patients suffering from personality disorders presents a challenge to mental health practitioners across all settings, and some research-findings are briefly referred to.

Chapter 4 addresses the clinical challenges of therapy by recounting the case of 'Harry' in detail. The description of his psychotherapy over time provides an opportunity to look at some aspects of technique with narcissistically damaged individuals. The split between the 'helpless maiden' and the 'insensitive brute' is explored as a chronic conflict between parts of the self, and as a dynamic between patient and therapist.

Chapter 5 offers an extremely condensed and simplified look at some of the major ways the concept of narcissism has evolved in the years since Freud's original work. It concludes with some comments about narcissistic disorder in Jung's personality, and the impact this had on his work and the evolution of psychoanalysis.

CHAPTER ONE

The Story of Narcissus: a psycho-sexual dynamic

Most stories have many versions, and the Greek myths concerning Narcissus and Echo are no exception. The most familiar version of the myth of Narcissus is that recorded in Ovid's *'Metamorphoses'*. The tale was re-told in modern language by Robert Graves (1981), and this version closely follows his:

Narcissus was a Thespian, the son of the blue nymph Leiriope, whom the River-god Cephisus had once encircled with the windings of his streams and ravished. The seer Teiresias told Leiriope, the first person ever to consult him, 'Narcissus will live to a ripe old age, provided that he never knows himself.' Anyone might excusably have fallen in love with Narcissus, even as a child, and when he reached the age of sixteen, his path was strewn with heartlessly rejected lovers of both sexes; for he had a stubborn pride in his own beauty. One day Narcissus sent a sword to his most insistent suitor, Ameinius, who killed himself on Narcissus' threshold, calling on the gods to avenge his death. Artemis heard the plea and ruled that Narcissus should fall in love, but that love's consummation should be denied him.

Among his lovers was the nymph Echo, who could no longer use her voice, except in foolish repetition of another's words. Her muteness was a punishment by the Goddess Hera, because Echo had distracted her attention with long stories so that she did not notice her husband Zeus's nymphs getting away.

One day when Narcissus went out to net stags, Echo stealthily followed him through the pathless forest, longing to address him, but unable to speak first. At last Narcissus, finding that he had strayed from his companions, shouted: "Is anyone here?"

"Here!" Echo answered, which surprised Narcissus since no one was in sight.

"Come!"

"Come!"

"Why do you avoid me?"

"Why do you avoid me?"

"Let us come together here!"

"Let us come together here!" repeated Echo, and joyfully rushed from her hiding place to embrace Narcissus. Yet he shook her off roughly and ran away. "I will die before you ever lie with me!" he cried. "Lie with me!" Echo pleaded. But Narcissus had gone.

At Donacon he came upon a spring, clear as silver, and never yet disturbed by cattle, birds or wild beasts or even by branches dropping off the trees that shaded it. As he cast himself down, exhausted, on the grassy verge to slake his thirst, he fell in love with his reflection and lay gazing enraptured into the pool, hour after hour. When, presently, he tried to embrace and kiss the beautiful boy who confronted him, he recognised it was himself. How could he endure both to possess and not to possess? Torn by grief, he knew at least that his other self would remain true to him, whatever happened.

Echo, still watching, grieved with him. Although she had not forgiven Narcissus, when she saw him plunge a dagger into his breast, she sadly echoed his dying words "Ah, youth, beloved in vain, farewell!" Where his blood soaked the earth, up sprang a white Narcissus flower with its red corolla. Echo, pining for her lost love, wasted away until only her voice remained to haunt the lonely woods.

Traditionally, the myth has been read as a moral fable about the tragedy of Narcissus. It depicts a tragic stalemate, and this provides the clue that the myth is describing a universal condition. The characters of Narcissus and Echo are symbolic of a drama that has been played out by humans over millennia. Although a mythical narrative cannot be brought as 'evidence' in support of clinical discoveries, the characters of Narcissus and Echo illuminate particular pathological defences. Their interaction represents an intrapsychic dilemma, a profound split, which is not resolved. Both characters are archetypal, larger-than-life. Their actions and emotions are absolute. Each is a catalyst for the other; to view the actions of one without consideration for the other is equivalent to describing a marriage from the viewpoint of one spouse only.

Narcissus' insensitive rejection and Echo's adhesive identification both express failures to negotiate a crucial turning point in human growth. In healthy development identification with, and introjection of, the object is flexible and progressive. Jungian theory understands human psychic development as a rhythmic continuum, encompassing merger, separation and re-merger.

Archetypal splits are usually addressed during family interactions and rendered human-sized. Myths and tales from all cultures deal with this issue. For most young children, the idealisation and the ferocity in 'fairy-tales' makes sense in terms of their own blissful or murderous fantasies and impulses. It is a relief that these have been understood and described by adults, especially by parental figures. Often, the tales have a moral intention ("you'll get your come-uppance!") arousing consciousness of guilt and punishment for sins. If the paranoid-schizoid anxieties and defences are met with understanding, a depressive capacity for concern arises.

When the maternal figure has been able to accept her child's dependence, and encourage separation from her appropriately, it is likely that the child will gradually be able to progress toward independence unencumbered by excessive anxiety. If not, the child may develop pseudo-independent defensive structures designed to avert intimacy. One classic pattern is that of omnipotent role reversal, when the child may attempt to nurture a failing parent. As adults, these people remain unable to gain much-needed love, attention and admiration, and may hold chronic grudges against 'fate'.

Punishment by 'the gods' is a powerful theme in the myth: both Narcissus and Echo are cursed with suffering. Narcissus is an arrogant young man and, although aware of his physical, external beauty, he is self-conscious without being self-aware. No one is good enough for him and he reacts to love with contempt and cruelty. He treats people as things, to be used and discarded, as though they have no feelings. When Ameinius dies, Narcissus does not care, but in the words of the old rhyme "is made to care".

Unable to empathise with others, to accept loss or to mourn their loss, Narcissus feels neither depression nor anxiety. But there is a price to pay for this failure of compassion: Narcissus is cursed to fall in love - in vain - and to experience the frustration and loss he has caused others to suffer; to feel, himself, the anguish of unrequited love. Only when he feels longing and reaches out for his beloved reflection does he "know himself". Unable to bear the frustration, Narcissus kills himself.

Although Narcissus appears callous and uncaring (schizoid), in the end he suffers acutely. Those hours at the pool, 'drinking in' his reflection, may appear to be merely an expression of self-love, but this also illustrates a defensive retreat within which the pain of separateness can be denied. Narcissus' inability to recognise himself when he gazes into the forest pool suggests developmental difficulty in infancy. When things go well, the mother's gaze mirrors back the infant to him or herself so that a strong sense of self and a healthy body-ego are established. Without the attentions of a 'good enough' mother, the infant has to relate to others from an intellectual or 'false' self constructed in his mind. As for Narcissus, a patient's sudden recognition of his or her previous state of total isolation can be crushing and dangerous.

Echo has also been punished for misusing her burgeoning sexuality, having tried to distract Hera's attention from Zeus' sexual dalliance with the nymphs. She is cursed by the goddess/mother with the inability to initiate relationships; her sexual power is taken away, and she suffers impotence, humiliation and rejection. Unable to approach and speak to Narcissus, she seizes the opportunity to misinterpret his wish to "come together here" to coincide with her own erotic desires, rushing out of hiding as if he has offered an invitation to a tryst. Her "masochistic fidelity only reaffirms Narcissus in his view that she is no more than a mirror and a pathetic creature" (Hamilton, 1982, pp. 128-9). Of course, she is brutally rebuffed, having tried to manipulate him into an entanglement he had neither expected nor sought. In the attempt to meet her needs, she controls rather than negotiates with him. Echo's manipulation of Narcissus results from muteness. After his rejection, Echo is engulfed by melancholia, falling into anxiety and self-absorbed rumination. Echo's silence in relation to the unattainable other illustrates the eternal repetitive damage, which ensues from narcissistic injury.

Echo's response to the rejection is characteristic of those suffering from pathological narcissism: in shame and humiliation, she withdraws whilst still anxiously clinging to her desire. Her mortification amounts to the death of creative potential, which may be manifested in a clinical setting by symptoms such as lethargy, despair and inability to take in anything good. Eventually Echo's body becomes painfully thin and wastes away until only her voice remains: the myth's warning about the ultimate prognosis of the condition if left untreated. It is not unusual to find patients suffering symptoms of anorexia and bulimia, in women especially. Hamilton (1982) has also linked Echo's plight with the profound grief that may be found at the core of patients with autistic disorders.

The interaction of Narcissus and Echo is set during adolescence, during which a young person begins to emerge from childhood dependence, through defiance, curiosity and experimentation, towards a relatively established adult identity. The figure of Narcissus is recognisable as an 'eternal adolescent' who wants excitement without commitment. During adolescence, many of the difficulties that have arisen during infancy and childhood are repeated. At the psychological heart of this stormy transition, lies a replay of pre-Oedipal and Oedipal tensions between the needs to identify and differentiate, control and negotiate, attract and reject. Issues of gender identification, and gender-role also complicate the picture.

In psycho-sexual development, the baby boy's first identification is with his mother, and in order to establish his gender identity the male infant must adjust to the not-female or not-mother bias, and form a positive identification with the father. For a girl, gender identity is built on her primary identification with her mother. The difficulties girls experience in establishing their feminine identities can arise from ambivalent experiences with mothers and distant fathers. Different developmental impulses, specific to male and female gender identification, can create a tension of opposites within the totality of the human psyche.

Although the myth describes the behaviour and reactions of an individual man and woman, their emotional interaction can be seen symbolically to represent an intrapsychic dynamic within the same individual which is not inherently allied with one gender or the other.

Jung came to believe that beneath the conscious (gendered) personality there lay another one of a quite different nature - an unconscious female within a man, and vice versa. He called these contra-sexual archetypes the anima (in man) and animus (in woman). These archetypes are 'realised' through projection onto another, usually of the opposite gender. Although they inevitably reflect characteristics from the collective social and political norms of any given time, Jung emphasised their timeless qualities that are not exclusive to one gender or the other (Hopcke, 1989). Jung was interested in providing a conceptual framework for understanding what each sex feels and thinks about the other, as a perceived opposite.

> "The role of anima and animus as soul images ...explains their particularly intense fascination: they are suffused with enigmatic hints of hidden depths which are in fact intimations of the unknown continent of our own interior being. The longing and desire we feel for those who personify them, whether actual love objects or imaginary figures...is a reflection of the longing we feel to be united with our 'other half', it is the thirst for wholeness and the union of opposites..." (Colman, 1998, p. 202)

Mothers and fathers, as well as social institutions and norms, reinforce certain gender role expectations. Little boys may come to deny the feminine or anima in themselves, in an effort to maximise their masculinity through self-sufficiency, ambition and competition. This model contrasts markedly with that for little girls. For the female child, the concept of *relationship* provides the ideal pattern for self development: a capacity for empathy, and responsiveness to others' needs is encouraged by mothers or caregivers in most cultures (Chodorow, 1985).

This perspective gives an added dimension to the mythical drama enacted by Narcissus and Echo. The inability of the two to engage in a relationship may be interpreted not only as pathology, but as an illustration of how different developmental impulses, specific to acculturated male and female gender identification, can become polarised within the human psyche, leading to a denial of the balancing contra-sexual component.

Patients coming for therapy frequently pose their problems in terms of unsatisfactory partners. The inability to appreciate the 'other' in a relationship often reflects the super-imposition of gender stereotyping onto narcissistic pathology. Patients often feel anguish, aware of some defect in their interactions with others, but powerless to change. There is frequently a deep sense of shame about their emptiness, but it is not a question of moral weakness. Narcissus' pseudo-independence and Echo's longing for merger both express a disturbance of the capacity to relate.

CHAPTER TWO

Some Clinical Examples

Alan

Alan, an advertising copy-writer in his early thirties, reluctantly agreed to consider psychotherapy at the suggestion of his mother. She was in the process of divorcing Alan's father, and Alan had been telephoning her several times a day in an agitated state. At the beginning of his two psychotherapy assessment sessions with Mrs A, Alan denied that he had any anxiety about the divorce himself, but expressed resentment about the emotional demands for support that he believed his mother was subtly placing upon *him* by *her* constant demands. He felt drained and exhausted by the constant hassle of helping her to sort things out.

Alan complained that his current girlfriend made similar demands for his attention. His male friends jokingly called him "a lady killer" because he had so many girlfriends. Whenever a relationship reached the point where it might involve commitment, he would quickly extricate himself and move on. He took some pride in this reputation but confessed that he had sometimes feared he might be gay: at least with blokes there were no emotional ties involved. Reflecting on his childhood, Alan described his parents as having been beautiful but distant. They had built up a highly successful fashion business, largely run by his energetic mother. They were both frequently abroad, and attention to Alan's needs had often been left to a series of nannies and au pairs. With pride, Alan described how he had taken on the responsibilities of 'housekeeper' in the family home, making shopping-lists and trying to do household repairs. To Mrs A, these tasks sounded quite inappropriate for his age, but she suggested to Alan that they must have given him a feeling of being needed and important. Alan agreed: although his parents had been much amused by his activities, he had felt superior to his sports-loving brother and two younger sisters, whom he dismissed as 'catwalk people'. Alan added scathingly that little had changed; he still had to look after things at home, for 'no-one else could do it'.

When the assessment phase came to an end, Alan decided that he wanted to continue psychotherapy on his own behalf. His weekly time and fees were agreed, and the meetings continued for the few weeks remaining until the Christmas holidays. Just before the break, however, Alan told Mrs A that he had to go away in January, to travel for work and a holiday. He said that he would telephone her about further sessions when he got back, as he was not sure of the date. Mrs A wanted to tell him off, as though he was an adolescent boy who decided to play rather than do his lessons/psychotherapy. This suggested that a transference/counter-transference re-enactment was taking place, within which she was being experienced as a demanding mother/girlfriend. She suggested that perhaps Alan felt he needed to get away from her for fear of being depended on and exploited by her as he often felt with his mother, and with other women. Alan agreed that this was true: he suspected Mrs A needed his money and had therefore trapped him into agreeing to attend regular sessions when what he really needed was to get away from it all. In the primitive realm, an individual's instinctual drive toward individuation is experienced as an urgent impulse to extricate itself from the maternal. Jung described the effort by the 'hero' to break maternal ties to primitive states in earliest infancy:

"The forward-striving libido which rules the conscious mind of the son demands separation from the mother, but his childish longing for her prevents this by setting up a psychic resistance that manifests itself in all kinds of neurotic fears – that is to say a general fear of life." (Jung, 1912b, p. 297)

As the therapy evolved it became clear that, although consciously Alan feared being trapped into demanding situations by an Echo-like female, unconsciously the needy, infantile, part of his psyche feared the absence of the maternal through her narcissistic self-absorption. This resulted in an identity confusion, and profound anxiety, defended against by narcissistic heroism ('no-one can cope but me'). When the break from therapy came along, threatening him with experiences of dependence and loss, Alan experienced the engulfing mother in projection onto Mrs A, as an intolerable obstacle to his personal freedom. He defended himself by flight.

Bridget

Bridget, a young woman in her thirties, came to her first assessment session powerfully dressed in a crisp blue business suit appearing cool, self-possessed and very poised. She came because her affair with a married man, a senior colleague in her project team at work, had reached a crisis. He wanted to tell his wife the truth about the affair, to be with Bridget properly. Although before, Bridget had believed she wanted this to happen she now felt doubtful and scared.

At school and university, Bridget's intelligence and laconic humour won her academic and social success but a repetitive pattern of failure in her love relationships began to emerge. She found that her initial attraction to a man would 'wear off' and within a few weeks she would become disillusioned and begin to treat him callously. If he lost interest in her, she would comfort herself that his 'lack of backbone' meant that he could not have been right for her.

Her report of her childhood as 'OK' did not quite tally with the distressing description of her mother who had several mental breakdowns. Bridget had turned to her father for love, but he was over-attentive, to the point of being physically intrusive. As a young girl she became careful about making sure she did not 'encourage' him. Bridget felt that her mother had envied her father's attachment to her, and punished her for it by sending her to boarding school. Bridget quickly learned, as she said, to 'look after herself', and 'never relied on her parents again'.

Similarly, in therapy, Bridget was unable to credit her therapist with any power that she, herself, lacked. She could not figure out why she could not solve the problem by herself. She could not allow in the therapist's concern. She perceived interpretations about her love affair representing a repetition of the frightening Oedipal triangle as envious attacks, which she defended herself against with cool disdain and mocking comments.

Early in the therapy Bridget reported a dream in which *she was inside a fortress or castle, and felt relief because she was completely safe from any outside intrusion. Then she noticed that there were no doors or windows in the walls, and realised that she was a prisoner.* This powerful image illustrated both the protective and persecutory aspects of her narcissistic defence.

When her lover decided after all to end the affair, Bridget accepted his decision with apparent equanimity, but in therapy she raged at his betrayal. This represented a turning point because she was surprised to realise that all the time she had been unconsciously dependent on his desire for her. She 'looked in the mirror' and saw the ruthlessness of her own wish to be the one who held the power. She felt shame about the sadistic heartlessness of her callous treatment of him.

These events evoked memories of how she turned away from her parents, especially her father, when she was sent away to school. Bridget began to allow herself to feel the intense pain of that separation, and mourn the loss of love she had been deprived of as a result. She could then articulate the fear aroused by her lover's emotional dependence, and express despair about her own capacity to love and be loved. Her therapist, however, able to make a feeling connection with her for the first time, knew that there was hope.

Chandit

Chandit, a young single man of twenty-five, brought himself to a work-place counselling service at the suggestion of his boss, who had noticed that often he sat looking into space, and was very slow in performing even simple tasks. Chandit explained to the counsellor that he was extremely self-conscious and shy. He was often preoccupied with fears that people were watching and criticising his appearance. Believing that he detected racism and contempt from colleagues made him determined to prove them wrong. He was spending increasingly long hours at work, hoping that he would gain recognition for his competence, but 'they' did not seem to notice. This persecutory anxiety was debilitating. He had become so paralysed that often a whole day would pass without him exchanging a word with anyone.

Nevertheless, Chandit confided a private feeling that he believed himself to have been blessed with unusual mathematical gifts, although his rather routine job did not provide him with much opportunity to display his talents. He sometimes felt superior to his colleagues, though explained that he had to be careful to hide this.

Chandit described how, as a little boy, he had constantly tried to please his mother by trying to be the perfect child. His mother had seemed always to be unhappy, pining for her home and family in India. Acutely aware of her distress, he sided with her in blaming his often-absent father for her misery. Father, when present, seemed to be contemptuous of him, and so Chandit was surprised and proud that father gave him the title deeds to the family house when he was still a teenager. Chandit was gratified that his father had vested him with such responsibility for the family security and diligently studied accounting to make sure he carried out his task well. He had been devastated and mortified to discover, when he left college, that in reality his father had made this apparent gift only to evade paying tax.

During his assessment session, the counsellor was concerned that Chandit might be in the early stages of a psychotic breakdown and arranged for him to be seen by a psychiatrist. He was given some medication, and the psychiatrist recommended that regular therapy sessions should be organised in the hope that Chandit's mental state would improve and a complete breakdown could be avoided.

In his early therapy sessions Chandit felt strongly that he was being watched and criticised. He would carefully wipe his shoes in an effort to maintain the perfection he thought was required. It was difficult for him to understand that whatever he said or thought was acceptable to his therapist, Mrs C, and potentially valuable. No-one had ever seemed to be as interested in him before. The attention soon 'went to his head' and he gradually revealed a fantasy that his case was of special interest to Mrs C, and that he was therefore being offered more sessions than her other patients. This defensive fantasy, acting as a counter-balance to his feeling of being 'small', gave him an illusion of control.

One day he discovered that in fact his treatment was 'pretty average' and feelings of worthlessness and of being discriminated against by Mrs C took over. This disillusionment, a repetition of the traumatic betrayal by his father, resulted in severe physical pain, which he described as feeling like a 'hole in his chest'. His narcissistic pain, experienced somatically, represented a double castration: the loss of power associated with Oedipal damage, and the loss of belief in the good therapist/breast with which he had been identified.

Whilst believing that he possessed exceptional abundance (Narcissus), at the same time Chandit's self-esteem was so fragile that it had collapsed at the realisation that in reality he was just like everyone else. This depressive collapse could not be expressed in words and, just as in his workplace, Chandit became profoundly silent (Echo).

Chandit's continuing relationship with a narcissistically vulnerable father had emphasised and intensified the splitting of infancy (Manzano, Palacio Espasa & Zilkha, 1999). His father's 'gift' of the title deeds had exacerbated the grandiose fantasies that bolstered up his aptitude for mathematics. But once in the everyday situation of office work, Chandit became puzzled and frustrated: if he was superior, why was he not sought after socially and, professionally, and given the credit he deserved? This inconsistency eventually brought him into therapy where he was helped to manage the, to him profound, humiliation of being merely human.

Whilst fearing ordinary dependence on others, the narcissistically damaged personality requires constant supplies of admiration, which never feel sufficient. Failures on the part of others to provide desperately needed support and positive mirroring throw the individual into torments of self-doubt. This internal dynamic is sometimes at the root of a narcissistic withdrawal.

David

David was a twenty-year-old man who came for urgent help in the final year of his art school degree in photography. He found himself unexpectedly likely to fail having lost interest in studying when his girlfriend, Emma, moved out without explanation. He was at a loss to understand why she had left him, but his therapist, Mr D, was *not* surprised when he learnt that David had sent her a note that he would be away on a six weeks' fashion shoot, enclosed with a Valentine's Day card. Mr D was unable to restrain a sharp comment indicating that the 'Valentine' had been insensitive, but he soon realised that his comment had made no dent in David's self-esteem. On the contrary, he arrogantly defended himself by saying that in his view he had every right to his 'independence'.

Untroubled by any doubts about the correctness of his own behaviour, David had embarked on a series of short-term liaisons with other women. He had believed that Emma's jealousy would be aroused and she would return to him; when she did, no longer be distracted by anger, he would be able to complete his degree successfully. It became clear that his strategy was not working, and he tried to get advice from Mr D about other ways to get Emma back. He was unable to study because his mind was full of rage towards Emma. He enquired angrily, "well, what do women want?" He said that if Emma did return to him now he might reject her, to hurt her as she had hurt him.

Exploration of David's history revealed that he had been taken into care at the age of eight after his mother had produced a stillborn baby brother and become seriously depressed. David had seemingly had no reaction to this separation from his mother, or the loss of the baby, though he admitted that he had never been as close to his mother afterwards. Throughout his life, David had remained unable to experience any of the feelings associated with loss until this crisis with Emma.

Following a long weekend break from therapy, David reported having felt weepy and anxious 'for no good reason'. He threatened to cut short his therapy because it was 'pointless' if it just made him feel worse. For the first time, Mr D found that he felt empathy for David. Mr D helped David to understand that his wish to attack the therapy was natural because he was so frightened of feeling again the pain of his childhood loss.

David was able to take this interpretation of his grief and find within himself some of the warmth that had existed with his mother before the traumatic separation. He came to see how he had identified Emma with his abandoning mother, and had been testing her commitment with his cruel 'Valentine'. He was able to apologise to her with feeling, for the pain he had caused her, and she agreed to try again.

David had been unable to imagine Emma's likely feelings of rejection on receiving the 'Valentine' because he could not see beyond his own concerns. Like Narcissus, he expected her to just 'be there' for his use and, like Echo, she had been unable to articulate her own needs. David regarded her as a thing to be manipulated with strategies, but in her absence was able to 'see himself' and to suffer the pangs of unattainable love.

This example illustrates a process that Jung called *enantiodromia*: a feeling taken to extremes turns into the opposite. If a one-sided position dominates conscious life, then the opposite attitude is stored up in the unconscious and will eventually break through. The ability to recognise and work with this principle can help a therapist to anticipate psychic shifts and to promote integration. Many narcissistically-wounded patients, like David, vow to 'never trust anyone again', and unconsciously set out to prove themselves right. Their partners' and therapists' inevitable failures bring renewed recrimination and hatred, but also a masochistic pleasure in holding a grudge. This perverse pleasure must be given up in order for depressive empathy and concern to be experienced.

Elisabeth

Elisabeth was a strikingly thin Swedish woman in her late thirties. She sought psychotherapy to try and increase her body-weight because she and her boyfriend wanted to have a child, but through anorexia her periods had stopped. Apart from food restriction, Elisabeth followed a punishing exercise regime. When she put on any weight, Elisabeth felt such hatred for herself that she would be driven to harm herself in other ways. Her upper-arms and thighs bore many scars inflicted by self-cutting, and she explained that this would relieve the unbearable feeling of badness inside.

Her parents had divorced when Elisabeth was five years old. Her father had remarried soon afterward to a much younger woman, and child support payments were erratic. Her mother had become an alcoholic. Ten years later, aged fifteen, Elisabeth returned home from school to find her mother unconscious on the kitchen floor. It was decided that the mother could no longer look after her, and Elisabeth went to stay with her father, stepmother and step-siblings. As soon as she could leave school, Elisabeth got a job and moved abroad to study.

In therapy, Elisabeth appeared to be philosophical about her parents' betrayal of her basic trust. As she saw it, having to leave her mother had instilled in her a sense of autonomy, and had required her to develop an impressive array of organisational skills for which she was grateful. She was highly valued at work in the travel industry, and was paid accordingly.

At weekends she was often accompanied by her boyfriend on trips abroad, and returned wearing the chic designer clothes he bought for her. These clothes gave a quite false impression of mature femininity, which she could only copy but did not feel. As Elisabeth expressed it, 'her body had grown up without her.'

Characteristically, Elisabeth worked hard during the initial period of her therapy with Dr E, conscientiously bringing 'appropriate' material her weekly sessions. She showed a meticulous respect for boundaries in terms of payment of fees and timekeeping. She never protested about interruptions in the therapy and would express polite puzzlement that Dr E placed such importance on them.

Two or three weeks before every scheduled break, Elisabeth would find that she 'had to' go away on a work assignment. Returning to therapy on the appointed day following a break, she would patiently listen to Dr E's interpretations: that in an effort to avoid painful feelings of dependency, she left Dr E in the same way that she had experienced being left as a child. Elisabeth learned to provide her own, quite plausible, interpretations and in this way would sometimes manage to silence Dr E.

One day she returned from a Christmas break, and reported the following dream:

Her father had found a small bird in the house, flying around in a panic. Inexplicably he beat the hapless bird to death with a tennis racket. It was a female carrying eggs. Elisabeth had been extremely distressed by his behaviour, but her father was seemingly unmoved.

This depiction of Elisabeth's attacks on her body and femininity was startling. Elisabeth acknowledged that she identified herself with the small brown bird, but was shocked when Dr E suggested that part of her was also the murderous attacker of her own femininity. This dream brought memories of her father's contempt for 'big women'. After leaving her mother's home, Elisabeth had learned to please him by enhancing her boyish qualities.

The bright-plumaged persona that had disguised her desolation became less necessary, and Elisabeth began to come to sessions in tracksuits and trainers with little or no make-up. She found she no longer sought the admiring glances of men in her office or at parties; nor did she enjoy provoking the envy of female acquaintances, which had boosted her self-esteem in the past. Gradually she became less voluble and during some sessions she would cry silently. The pain of her grief was so intense that often she was unable to speak at all.

There were a series of losses in Elisabeth's early life: the breakdown of the parental couple, her father's departure, and then her mother's alcoholism. One of the consequences of divorce for children is damage to the symbolic unity of parental imagos, which sets the stage for future difficulties in integration. Elisabeth remembered that, as a little girl, she had believed that her father went away because she was bad and unlovable. Within the logic of the infantile inner world, the rift in her parents' marriage was her fault. Her mother's apparent indifference to her husband's departure meant that Elisabeth could not admit her own love for and loss of father for fear she would lose mother's love as well.

When such traumas occur during childhood, aspects of the Mother or Father archetypes, particularly the negative ones, are unmediated, and may even be reinforced, by experience. Erich Neumann (1966) described how a distress-ego takes over to try and manage anxiety through premature independence. This gives rise to the characteristic false maturity in adulthood that Elisabeth had presented with. The distress-ego can only, of course, operate with the mental capacity of the child at the time of the trauma. This therefore involves primitive 'solutions', such as splitting and projection.

Elisabeth unconsciously experienced her mother's collapse, during her own adolescence, as an envious attack on her emergent feminine self. Like Echo, the young girl became unable to express or enjoy her sexuality. Elisabeth 'identified with the aggressor' and began to assault her own body in ways that would prevent or obscure her sexual maturity. Elisabeth's corrosive self-contempt manifested in a constant barrage of nagging self-criticism, denigration of her assets and accomplishments, and in self-mutilation. This had been enhanced by the unconscious narcissistic misogyny of her father.

In therapy, Elisabeth was slowly able to relinquish her attacks on the libidinal self and turn towards Mrs E as a 'life giver' (Symington, 1993). The therapeutic couple could then work together on the creation of a more authentic self.

Flora

This middle-aged woman was an in-patient on a psychiatric ward, diagnosed with psychotic depression following an overdose. Flora's mother had died when she was not yet two. Her father, unable to cope with such a young child as well as four others under ten, sent Flora to live with an aunt and uncle in a distant part of Africa. She did not attend her mother's funeral, nor was Flora's mother ever mentioned in her new home, for fear of upsetting her.

A childhood memory illustrates her particular kind of isolation. Flora (aged about four) and her aunt were walking over a wooden bridge connecting their small offshore island to the mainland. Although holding tightly to her aunt's hand, Flora was convinced that she would fall through the gap between the wooden planks of the bridge to the green ocean below. Her aunt's practical demonstration that Flora's foot was too big to go through the gaps between the planks failed to allay the child's distress. Her irrational terror represented the nameless dread of 'falling forever' into the depths of unconsciousness or death.

Having been denied the crucial experience of mourning for her lost family, Flora was unable to move on to negotiate important steps in separation and individuation. One day, Flora's aunt and uncle went on a short trip without her, leaving her in the care of a neighbour whom she did not trust. Flora 'knew' the woman was lying when she said that her aunt and uncle would return to fetch her, and was firmly convinced that another set of parents had disappeared forever. In order to manage her terror, Flora's psyche dissociated, and she constructed a delusional fantasy world where she could magically control the comings and goings of adults. On the surface, she was therefore able to appear unconcerned, self-contained and compliant. After a few days, her aunt and uncle did come to get her, but Flora retreated into a cupboard and refused to go home. The aunt interpreted this as an expression of the child's anger with her for going away, but it was also fear, for their return had breached Flora's carefully constructed defensive 'castle' by showing that she could not really control anybody.

These early experiences reverberated throughout Flora's adult life. After entering a religious order, she worked as a volunteer in various refugee camps throughout Africa, helping others who had also experienced catastrophic separation from their own families. As a young adult, she effectively put her life 'on hold'. In mid-life, she had been criticised for her moralistic and judgmental attitudes and she was sent to the UK by her order. Only then did the omnipotent defence break down as it had in childhood, closing her into a cupboard of debilitating depression and encapsulated rage. Prevented from continually repeating the reparative actions of caring for others, Flora gradually saw that her own inner world contained only 'dead' objects. The feelings of grief and guilt were intolerable, and Flora made a serious suicide attempt and was admitted to hospital.

It took many months of hospital care before Flora could begin to allow herself to be helped. One day, Flora was asked during an art therapy group to visualise an image of herself as a creature or plant. Without effort, into her head came the picture of a wild rose bush, abundantly flowering, delicately fragrant but, as in the nature of wild roses, rambling and in her view unacceptably untidy. In the fantasy, Flora tidied it up by uprooting the entire bush and throwing it over the wall of the garden in which it was innocently blooming. When she revealed this vision to the other members of the group, she was very hurt when they told her that her 'tidying up' was an attack on her own creativity. Flora's predicament can be understood in terms of 'anti-narcissism' (Bollas, 1989, p. 167) in that potentially valuable elements in herself and others had to be destroyed.

Flora's therapist, Mrs F, understood that the rose bush was a self-image and that Flora had been describing the experience of being uprooted and evicted from the shelter of home when her mother had suddenly and tragically died. Unable to comprehend the abandonment by her much-loved and loving father and mother, the infant concluded that she was a bad child who was being punished for being unruly. Such distrust of one's own nature arouses many fears and distortions of self-perception. Flora had until now been locked within an unshakeable pattern, which had isolated her from others, killed off her own creativity, and cut her off from sources of help.

Gill

Gill's first communication to her therapist, Miss G, was that her life had totally lost meaning since her husband left her and their two children had been taken into care as a result of her addiction to hard drugs. This was a terrible narcissistic wound for Gill, who had reacted by increasing her drug taking to dangerous levels in an effort to 'anaesthetise' herself.

Gill had married a long-distance lorry-driver when she was twenty-two. She told Miss G that she had quite liked her 'Navy marriage' in which it was inevitable that the couple would be apart for long periods and they had two children in quick succession. But after her husband was made redundant they began taking drugs. Gill explained that, at first, she had done so to 'keep her husband company', but then she could not stop. She had joined Narcotics Anonymous, but was contemptuous of the NA meetings, which fostered openness between people, since allowing anyone close was 'mad'. She found other people's open emotional vulnerability 'silly' and humiliating. Gill found it terrifying to have close relationships, even with the children. She had continued to use drugs, and was on a permanent 'high' until her husband left and she lost the children. Following this she returned, humiliated, to live in her childhood home.

Her childhood memories were few but telling. Gill's father had developed a neuronal disorder and had to retire at an early age. No repairs were ever made to the large ill-kept family home because mother was too busy and father was too ill. He was confined to a wheelchair, was withdrawn and ill-tempered, often refusing to speak. Mother had to work, and so care of her father and younger sister often fell to Gill, who had to cook the family meals every day after school.

Although Miss G could see that the family atmosphere during Gill's childhood had been miserable, and her parents at times gravely exploitative, Gill clung to the belief that they had been a happy family. Gill admired her mother tremendously, for having managed to keep the family together despite all their problems. Now, back at home at the age of thirty, she quickly returned to her childhood role of helper and nurse.

Before the first long break in therapy, Gill announced to Miss G one evening that she had taken some 'uppers' and had stopped eating. In a light, careless tone, she explained that she could not be bothered to prepare things for herself and the corner shop had no Bakewell tarts, her favourite food. Miss G was concerned by Gill's manic reaction to the forthcoming break and suggested that not eating was an expression of her rage and despair about being left alone to care for herself. This interpretation was confirmed when Gill retorted: "Why should I have to feed myself?" Miss G realised that, in the transference, she was representing a cruelly depriving breast-mother who did not care whether Gill 'starved'.

Miss G wanted to allow Gill the fullest possible expression of her rage but, aware of Gill's capacity to act out, could not be sure that Gill had the ego-strength necessary to contain it without damaging herself further. With Gill's agreement, she therefore made contact with the GP to alert him to Gill's vulnerability, and it was arranged that a Community Psychiatric Nurse would 'baby-sit' while she was away.

On Miss G's return, Gill brought an expensive gift for her. Miss G opened the package but kept it on the table between them, indicating that it was a matter for discussion. It soon became clear that Gill was mystified and hurt that Miss G had failed to reciprocate by not bringing her a present. The failed exchange of presents represented the maternal mirroring that Gill longed for but that had, from her point of view, been withheld. Gill wept as she described how the same thing often happened at home with her parents. Although as a woman Gill knew that she no longer needed parental approval, she could not stop her child-self from trying to please them.

Gill began to express anger about how her parents 'fed off her': demanding help and attention but seldom reciprocating. She recalled that as a teenager she sometimes felt resentful about the demands on her and longed for a cuddle or a 'thank-you'. When the desired affectionate gestures were not forthcoming, she would turn to Bible stories that promised spiritual reward for selfless devotion. Gill would pray diligently for atonement for her 'selfishness', and came to believe that she might even be able mend her father if only she strove hard enough to be good.

The ability to relinquish unrealistic ideals and to mourn for the lifelong losses that had been suffered – in fact, to accept disillusionment – was a sign that Gill's narcissistic defences were beginning to yield. She became able to participate in her NA group fully, and to master her addiction.

Summary

In these clinical examples we have explored some of the major dilemmas confronting the narcissistically damaged patient in therapy:
- Fear of and longing for dependency
- Problems with gender identity and sexuality
- Impairment of the capacity for mourning and empathy
- Sado-masochistic object relating

In the next chapter, we address some of the clinical challenges presented by these patients in terms of assessment, engagement and containment within the therapeutic relationship.

CHAPTER THREE

Manifestations of Narcissism

The behaviour and psychological states covered by the term "narcissism", represent a spectrum of intensity and pathology. At one end lies the normal solipsism of infancy and early childhood and the self-absorption natural in bereavement. At the other extreme lies the loss of contact with external reality associated with psychosis, and the dangerous inability to empathise of the psychopathic personality. Between these two extremes lie the narcissistic disorders that are in some way disabling, but amenable to psychotherapeutic treatments.

Some clinicians have the view that narcissistic disorder should be considered as a dimension of psychopathology which cuts across all diagnostic categories. Richard Stolorow has offered a "functional" definition as follows:

"Mental activity is narcissistic to the degree that its function is to maintain the structural cohesion, temporal stability, and positive affective colouring of the self representation." (Stolorow, 1986, p.198)

If there is an assumption that narcissistic phenomena will be present to some degree in every case, the question then arises: what is the degree of narcissistic disturbance within this patient, and how disabling is it for them?

Some manifestations of narcissistic disorder in everyday life

At home:
Severe narcissistic damage may result in an 'almost total incapacity to establish genital and tender relations with any other human being' (Kernberg, 1976b). More commonly, those who suffer with narcissistic pathology typically make **narcissistic object choices**, a term used to indicate a love-object based on the model of the subject's own self. The denial of the object as a separate being leads to **exploitation of, and inability to empathise with, the other**. There is likely to be profound **ambivalence about sexual relationships**, and sexual perversions such as sado-masochism may be reported. Because the narcissist does not truly believe in his or her lovableness; they may resort to **seduction**, and their partner then has a feeling of being used or manipulated. This situation can mimic the process of falling in love, but often leads to a cycle of **destructive jealousy**.

The narcissistic sufferer **is frequently attracted to people who are felt to be withholding.** The fact that the object is attractive or valued by others inspires in them a desire to possess, but induces strong **feeling of helplessness.** The desired object may be clung to, despite its incapacity to provide, so that the partners are **split into 'innocent victim' and 'cruel perpetrator'.** The everyday wear and tear of an ongoing primary relationship with its minor slights, misunderstandings, and lapses of care and attention often lead to **unexpected rages** which can be quite overwhelming for both patient and family.

At work:

Narcissistic grandiosity cuts across social and economic boundaries, and is not restricted to the consulting room by any means; in fact it flourishes in all cultures in everyday life, in the workplace, in the media, on the sporting field. Because our Western society highly prizes hard work and self-sacrifice, the sufferer may seem well adapted socially and professionally. The 'successful' narcissist, who earns enough recognition and admiration, will rarely seek therapy (Asper-Bruggisser, 1987). This kind of narcissistic patient usually presents for help only when the narcissistic defences are failing to sustain self-esteem against feelings of inner emptiness and difficulties in relationships at work, at home and socially.

Narcissistically damaged children are often high achievers, and may become very hard working adults, conscientious to a fault and bound by high moral principles. Despite their best intentions, however, they often alienate others with their **arrogant attitude**. They may exude an air of **self-importance** as though they believe that they are special or superior, and have an **excessive need for admiration**. This is accompanied by **a tendency to devalue the contributions of others.** They may nurture a **sense of grievance and injustice** if the vital narcissistic supplies of appreciation are not forthcoming. **Criticism leaves them feeling humiliated** and puzzled, because they have tried so hard to do well.

Socially:

In order to bolster feelings of self-esteem, narcissistic sufferers may indulge in **hyperactive socialising**. Examples would include non-stop clubbing, promiscuity, and extravagant present giving. Unable to accept physical limitations, some people may neglect their physical needs, self-harm, have eating disorders, or behave so recklessly that it amounts to suicidal behaviour.

Narcissistic vulnerability leads to painfully **envious feelings** for those whom they intuitively know to possess a good internal object, often regarded as 'having an easier time in life'. They respond to actual or perceived social failure with **social withdrawal** and **depression**. This may be accompanied by **fantasies of a magical solution**: there may be constant plans to change partner, job, or to emigrate and 'start a new life'.

Gender issues

Much of the psychoanalytic work on narcissism has related to the character of Narcissus alone, rather than including that of Echo. This *may* mean that women are less prone to narcissistic disturbance than men, or more likely, that the manifestations of narcissism in women tend to be different – more 'Echo' than 'Narcissus'. Most of the early cases studied in depth were men and this has led to an emphasis on diagnostic criteria such as grandiose fantasies, pseudo-independence, fits of rage and paranoia in the face of perceived criticism.

Kernberg (1976a) differentiated between narcissistic women who have the "typical traits of coldness and exploitation", and "much better integrated masochistic women" who cling desperately to idealised men. Kernberg's differentiation obscures the significant narcissistic elements in masochistic women. Perhaps his view that they are not 'typical' explains the low number of female narcissists reported in his clinical investigations - at least before 1990. But as early as 1940 Annie Reich was exploring narcissistic disorder in women patients:

> "The submissive woman seems completely to have renounced her own [healthy *] narcissism. It is as if she had projected her narcissism onto the man; she develops a sort of megalomania in regard to him. In the magic of the unio mystica she finally regains through identification the narcissism which she

has renounced." (Reich, 1940, pp. 198-206)
[*added by current authors]

She goes on to describe how desires originally related to the mother can be intensely sexualised, resulting in perverse passivity aimed at commanding constant love and attention in relationships with men. Clinicians have continued to note that the condition of narcissism develops and expresses itself differently in men and women (eg. Richman & Flaherty, 1990).

These differences can be accounted for in terms of identification with 'Echo' rather than with 'Narcissus'. Diagnostic criteria taking Echo into account would include: the drive for fusion with an omnipotent object, **self-harm**, and **withdrawal** into quasi-autistic states. If the story of Narcissus and Echo describes *an emotional interaction within* the personality, the characteristics described cannot be inherently allied with one gender or the other. Thus, both aspects of the sadomasochistic narcissistic dynamic would be included.

Assessment for psychotherapy

Although there have been some excellent contributions in the field of assessment from psychoanalytic therapists (eg. Coltart, 1988; Hinshelwood, 1991; Josephine Klein, 1999 & 2002), approaches to assessment sessions tend to differ widely. Some therapists approach an initial interview as the first in a process they assume will be ongoing. Others consider the assessment process as a complete piece of work in itself.

Because narcissistic traits occur across a spectrum they are found in all people to varying degrees, and whether or not narcissistic problems are going to form a major element in a new patient's therapy is not always easy to determine.

A new patient may complain of difficulties with attending to duties and responsibilities, at work or college, psychosomatic symptoms or loss of meaning and direction in life. Each of these may be present as part of a normal experience such as bereavement, or of another disorder such as depression, so in order to discover whether or not they indicate narcissistic disturbance, it is necessary to pay attention to the patient's *attitude* to these symptoms. Do they **feel they always have 'bad luck'**, for example, or that they have been singled out for bad treatment and that the people in their lives always misunderstand them?

Narcissistic personalities are **frequently judgmental** by nature, and maintain high standards for themselves and others. Plagued by fantasies of perfection and ultimate control, their keen sense of justice can turn to **indignation and outrage** at the way the world has treated them. The therapist is therefore treated at first as a mirroring or idealised self-object, rather than as a separate and whole object.

The patient may believe that he or she is special and cannot really be understood by the therapist. The **belief in their specialness** will come into intense conflict with **a fear that their flaws will be revealed**. Although they long to be looked after, dependency and neediness mean weakness to the person who suffers from pathological narcissism who will go to great lengths to avoid **the humiliation of admitting a need** for others. Coming to a therapist thus involves painful **feelings of shame** (Wharton, 1990).

The patient will **secretly idealise and envy the therapist** for possessing the 'secret of happiness'. Efforts to get hold of this secret inevitably fail, because the patient does not have the capacity for relatedness within which things can be learnt from the other. Instead, **communication occurs primarily through projective identification**, which allows the patient to evacuate hated parts of the self into the therapist. The patient may turn against and **denigrate the therapist** with contempt. His or her efforts may seem to be directed towards making the therapist ineffective, interpretations being ignored, derided or appropriated as the patient's own.

Some possible contraindications

Why is it important for the clinician to be able to detect signs of narcissistic disorder, as the principal pathology, at the point of assessment? Psychotherapy involves at least a nascent capacity to symbolise. The **inability of the patient to think about his part in his downfall, active addictions to drugs or alcohol, and the inability to accept responsibility for criminal behaviour** indicate that acting out is likely to absorb the entire enterprise. Because such patients lack secure ego-boundaries they rely on external structures for containment. Often, breaks or changes in their care are experienced as intolerable and so they need a high level of consistency and reliability.

This has implications for the resources of the therapist at a given time. Working individually with narcissistic patients is often rather a heroic enterprise for the therapist may be called on to forego or suspend their own need for gratitude, and a shared sense of value for the work, for extended periods. Part of the assessment process needs to be whether the therapist has sufficient psychic space and energy to provide adequately for this patient who will at times be very draining on therapeutic resources.

The prospective therapist has to work within the demands and constraints of a particular setting: public or private sector, long or short-term, and these limitations may undermine the therapeutic treatment. The availability of support from family and friends, and the active co-operation of GP or psychiatrist, may be essential. Although medication may help by moderating their anxiety, the underlying problems often recur and so these patients often have recurrent contact with psychiatric services.

Narcissistic disorders in psychiatry

The psychotherapy profession has been ambivalent about the use of psychiatric classifications, fearing that such labels are unhelpful and may even be damaging for a patient.

Naturally, the emphasis is usually on the need to make a psychodynamic formulation, but it is sometimes vital to be able to relate this to a patient's psychiatric diagnosis.

Although descriptions of narcissistic personality disorder have for many years appeared in The Diagnostic and Statistical Manual of Mental Disorders (American Psychiatric Association, 1994), it is not used as a major diagnostic category in its own right. DSM-IV employs a multi-axial system in which the patient is assessed on five different scales or axes:

1) clinical disorders
2) personality disorders: long term patterns of impaired functioning through personality disorders or mental retardation
3) general medical conditions: any physical illness that might influence the patient's mental state or ability to function
4) psychosocial and environmental problems: significant stressful events within twelve months of the onset of symptoms
5) assessment of functioning: an overall measure of the patient's functioning at work and in daily life.

Narcissistic personality disorder comes within the broad category of **borderline personality disorders** and patients share some of the same traits. The term borderline is somewhat fluid, but most simply it describes patients whose difficulties lie on the borders of neurotic and psychotic symptomatology.

DSM-IV lists the following features of borderline personality disorder:

1) frantic efforts to avoid abandonment
2) unstable and intense relationships characterised by extremes of idealisation and devaluation
3) persistent unstable self-image or sense of self

4) impulsivity in two areas that are potentially self-damaging: spending, sex, substance abuse, reckless driving, binge eating
5) recurrent suicidal behaviour, gestures, threats, or self-mutilation
6) affective instability ie. intense irritability or anxiety
7) chronic feelings of emptiness
8) inappropriate intense anger or difficulty controlling anger
9) stress-related paranoid or dissociated symptoms

A borderline personality disorder patient will usually seek help with their chaotic, impulsive behaviour. Those suffering from narcissistic personality disorder may, by contrast, present themselves as relatively socially effective, having achieved some degree of worldly success. This means that they are more likely to be referred for psychotherapy than other borderline patients.

DSM-IV describes the patient with **a narcissistic personality disorder** as follows:

[The patient has] a pervasive pattern of grandiosity (in fantasy or behaviour), need for admiration, and lack of empathy, beginning by early adulthood and present in a variety of contexts, as indicated by five (or more) of the following:
1) a grandiose sense of self-importance
   (eg. exaggerates achievements and talents; expects to be recognised as superior without commensurate achievements)
2) is preoccupied with fantasies of unlimited success, power, brilliance, beauty, or ideal love
3) believes that he or she is "special" and unique and can only be understood by, or should associate with, other special or high-status people (or institutions)
4) requires excessive admiration

5) has a sense of entitlement, ie. unreasonable expectations of especially favourable treatment or automatic compliance with his or her expectations
6) is interpersonally exploitative, ie. takes advantage of others to achieve his or her own ends
7) lacks empathy: is unwilling to recognise or identify with the feelings and needs of others
8) is often envious of others or believes that others are envious of him or her
9) shows arrogant, haughty behaviours or attitudes.

Readers will note that these traits refer to 'Narcissus' rather than 'Echo'. The traits of 'Echo' are frequently, and mistakenly, ascribed to depression and treated accordingly. The more grandiose affectations of narcissistic patients can lead them to demand attention in extremely off-putting, high-handed ways. The patient may puzzle and infuriate helpers by his or her 'attention-seeking behaviour' and ingratitude. But no matter how arrogant such a person may appear, there is always an Echo-self that is being treated with the same disdain as the helpers, and that is seeking sympathetic recognition.

Within NHS psychotherapy services, resource constraints often limit what can be offered to once-weekly group or individual work, often with a trainee. Some research studies have proved that psychotherapy can lead to improvements for patients with personality disorders (see Bateman, 2000 and Siani & Siciliani, 2000). But although a weekly 'dose' of therapy may be sufficient to support the patient so that further crises can be averted, these weekly sessions alone may not be enough to initiate change (Agass, 2000). Treatments in NHS settings that have been proved to be particularly effective with these patients have involved a combination of therapies (White et al, 2001). Despite the obvious risks of splitting, these patients often benefit most from with medication and nursing input *combined with* individual or group psychotherapy.

The narcissistic patient may benefit especially from a homogeneous group, where they can spend some time in mutual support, than in the classic 'stranger' group of more neurotic patients who may be less defended (Hearst, 1988). Concurrent individual therapy may be able to help with their difficulties in inter-personal relationships as manifested within the group, provided the therapeutic team is working together closely.

CHAPTER FOUR

Therapeutic Challenges

"..chaos is come again..."
Othello, Act III

The tragedy of Shakespeare's Othello flows from his incapacity to know that he is truly loved. Even after he had won the beautiful Desdemona, he was tormented by self-doubt; how could she possibly love him, a rough old seaman? His clever but envious lieutenant, Iago, played on these doubts to destroy the couple. He whispered in Othello's ear 'evidence' of her unfaithfulness – just like the persecuting voice of an auditory hallucination. This voice meshed with Othello's doubts, and he was driven into a jealous rage during which he killed his beloved wife. Then, realising what he had done in his madness, that he had killed 'the thing he loved', he committed suicide.

When Othello was induced by Iago to suspect Desdemona of unfaithfulness, the bubble of their blissful union was pierced. His idealisation of her goodness collapsed, and this resulted in terrible destruction. The chaos he had known was inside himself 'came again' and was tragically enacted.

Moments of catastrophic suspicion such as this are common when working with a patient with narcissistic difficulties. Their core sense of self is extremely fragile, and easily shattered by everyday problems in living. Harry, whose case is discussed here in detail, experienced similar episodes of suspicion, and tested his objects to the edge of destruction.

Assessment

Harry was referred by his GP to Mr H, an experienced counsellor and trainee psychotherapist practising locally. At the end of his telephone call to make an appointment, Harry did not say goodbye but merely put the receiver down in a very business-like manner, leaving Mr H feeling rather snubbed. Harry arrived at the appointed hour. He was charming and affable, grasping Mr H's hand in a man-to-man clasp. Harry was in his late forties but looked youthfully fit and was trendily dressed.

Recently, Harry hadn't been sleeping well, and had begun to experience heart palpitations. It was his alarm about this that led him to contact his GP, who happened to be a golfing friend. Although medical tests had showed no physiological abnormalities to his heart, he was afraid that one of his rages would bring on a fatal heart attack. After checking that there was nothing organically wrong with his heart, the GP had suggested therapy. Harry doubted whether therapy would suit him, but was prepared to follow his friend's advice.

Harry's current partner, Lynn, had threatened to leave him if he could not find a way to spend more time with her. They had been arguing a lot and during these fights Harry often lost his temper, leading to palpitations. Afterwards, he could hardly bear to look at her 'miserable face'. Harry's self-confessed 'obsessional' work ethic had brought him some success and financial reward in business, but he had not been promoted as quickly as he had expected. Recently, Harry's business had been subject to a hostile take-over bid from a rival firm and he was threatened with redundancy. Lynn had urged him to grab the redundancy money and to 'make a killing' by investing the capital in a somewhat shady property development. Although tempted, Harry could not bring himself to take the risk.

In the past year a colleague at work had died suddenly of a heart attack. He had also recently lost his mother, to whom he had been close, from cancer. This had been a great shock, but he felt satisfied that he had handled his duties as executor efficiently. Harry believed that all problems in life could best be dealt with practically, without emotion. He subscribed to the motto of his management course: 'just do it!' Mr H drew attention to the fact that, not only was Harry's physical heart in trouble, but also his emotional 'heart', his feeling self, which did not know how to manage his experiences of loss.

Harry explained that he had learned to be pragmatic and disciplined from his father, a surgeon. He had always tried to emulate his father's surgical precision by adopting the attitude of an 'automaton' early in his life. This had helped him to cope after his parents' divorce when he was six years old. He vaguely remembered his parents' continual rowing, and his father moving out. His mother had 'always needed a lot of looking after', and as a boy he had often helped out with shopping and cooking. He frequently stayed away from school and, for fear of going back, would feign illnesses.

His mother quickly re-married 'for the sake of the child'. Harry loathed and feared his stepfather who was, he said, a bully who was particularly unsympathetic about the boy's bed-wetting and fear of the dark. The only other piece of childhood information Harry offered was that soon after he was born, his mother had been admitted to hospital with post-natal depression for about two months, during which time Harry had been looked after by a live-in nanny.

Towards the end of the assessment session, Harry asked a series of probing questions, trying to establish whether Mr H, a younger man, was sufficiently experienced to handle his particular problems. Mr H felt he was being interviewed for a job, and interpreted that Harry wanted to be sure he was in good hands – efficient hands, like his late father's. Harry received this with a wry smile, as though Mr H had scored a point over him. Mr H suggested that they might both need to think over the interview before deciding about beginning therapy, to which Harry replied (of course): 'let's just do it!' Harry reluctantly agreed to a compromise: a second assessment session to make the decision together.

This initial picture of Harry provided many clues to the probable underlying psychological difficulties. As Jeremy Holmes remarked in his review of attachment theory: "In the clinical setting the patient's narrative style and, especially, tone of voice provide a… clue to the state of their object relations" (Holmes, 2000, p.167). Harry was charismatic and intelligent, but there were indications of narcissistic disturbance – the shallowness of his emotional life, the need for admiration, and the robotic approach to life's challenges. He wanted to 'do' therapy like he could do a business deal.

The acute psychosomatic disruption experienced as heart palpitations might be linked with a reactivation of the traumatic loss of mother when he was only a few weeks old. Failures in infant care at such an early stage are often registered physically rather than mentally and are 'remembered' by the body. In the somatic realm, access to potentially healing phantasy may remain blocked. Joyce McDougall, writing about patients with psychosomatic illnesses, remarked on "…the difficulty – and perhaps the inadvisability – of engaging such patients in psychotherapy" (McDougall, 1989, p. 68).

Generally, narcissistic personality disorder patients have responded to care-taking failures in early childhood by setting up structures of self-care (Kalsched, 1996), such as Harry's 'automaton-self', that are resistant to change. The images Harry had presented were of a man who had used will-power and action to 'execute' self-discovery.

Mr H mused that the 'shady property deal' could represent a transference communication about mistrust of the therapeutic process and/or anxiety about the shadow elements Harry might discover in himself. What might be 'killed', if he entered therapy? Was there a danger that Harry might commit suicide if he came to 'know himself', as Narcissus did? There was also an image of damaged femininity that might grow out of control, like a cancer. Harry was experiencing some distress, but it remained a question whether he would be capable of mourning his lost objects and initiating an individuation process.

During his second assessment session, Harry confided that he had become impotent for the past few months. He said it had happened before with previous partners, and usually signalled the end of the line for that relationship. Usually, the impotence vanished as soon as he found some 'new blood' to excite him. Although Harry had never married, he had lived with several women, usually younger than himself. He enjoyed the women's admiration, and took pleasure in buying them expensive gifts. He told a lengthy story about buying an antique violin at auction for one who was a musician, "but of course", he concluded, "I know that money can't buy you love". He said that these women had all eventually 'let him down'; they always tried to change him, but he didn't know why. He had always believed that he had no real problems, other than being with the wrong woman! In response to their nagging, he would retaliate in various ways: with criticism, with silence, with verbal abuse, until they 'gave up' and left. He *had* thought that

Lynn was different, 'special'. After his mother's death, she had talked to him about his feelings; she'd had some counselling herself not long ago. He remembered Mr H's comment about his 'heart' being in trouble; it sort of made sense. He'd begun to feel he needed Lynn but now she, too, was angry with him. He couldn't go on like this.

Harry's need for a woman to make him feel unconditionally loved seemed likely to be related mostly to complex difficulties associated with his mother's depression. His defence against loss had been exacerbated by the identification with an absent or emotionally cruel father: "the absence of an effective father results in damage to the de-integrating self, or in other language results in narcissistic damage..." (Carvalho, 1982, p. 342).

It was a positive sign that, between Harry's first and second assessment interviews, he had held on to Mr H's observation about his feeling self being in trouble. Mr H and his supervisor also noted that, with Lynn, Harry was perhaps for the first time, acknowledging frightening feelings of dependence. Her support would be valuable since psychotherapy would involve an attempt to bring about separation from primitive mechanisms for coping with disillusionment and fear. For Harry, this would probably be felt as an extreme threat to his physical safety as well as to his psychic integrity. Because these patients have had to exert defensive control over childhood environments that felt mad and bad, their capacity for allowing a free flow of feeling, for separation, and concomitant mourning – for lost objects, 'happy childhoods' they never had, for life unlived – is severely compromised. Hr H's attempts to introduce the reality of interdependence would be likely to encounter fierce resistance or violent narcissistic withdrawal. Despite these misgivings, Mr H decided to offer twice-weekly ongoing therapy. Harry responded and agreed to the regular session times suggested. When Harry began therapy he, like most patients, had little context of psychological knowledge within which overwhelming feelings such as rage, fear and despair could be contained. For patients who are especially vulnerable to narcissistic wounding, psychotherapy is hard to bear.

Harry did not know how to 'play the game' of therapy. He had few conscious memories or images of childhood to bring, rarely remembered dreams, and believed only in the power of reason to resolve emotional difficulties. Rather than being remembered, Harry's painful history was re-enacted within relationships. Harry related to Lynn as though she could, 'if she chose', supply him with what he needed. The common thread between the moments that sparked his rage was that Lynn had failed to conform to his expectation – even if this expectation had been unconscious.

Establishing the Therapeutic Alliance

One evening, soon after his therapy began, Lynn arrived home an hour later than expected from work. This ignited his sexual jealousy. Although Lynn explained that the delay had really been unavoidable, Harry could not let it go. During the evening he questioned and harangued her: He accused her of having been with another man, someone who would satisfy her sexually. Finally, in a rage he physically pushed her out of their flat. This fight had again brought on severe chest pains. When the pain abated Harry went after Lynn and persuaded her to come back. He was terrified of losing her, he explained, but she should have avoided being late because she knew how it upset him.

In his session he tried to recruit Mr H's sympathy. But Mr H felt more sympathy for Lynn, and he could not contain expressions of disapproval about Harry's violence. Harry responded to this lack of support by saying: " I don't suppose you can have had another patient as messed up as me." Mr H suggested that Harry was already feeling 'let down' by him, as he did by other people. Harry retorted: "What you're saying doesn't seem to be making me feel better, anyway." He then went on to vent his frustration with other 'so-called professionals' who had not taken his chest-pain seriously enough, and just told him that he must change his life-style. "How can I change - just like that?" he said, snapping his fingers.

Harry expected his objects to be utterly reliable, to attend only to him, to love him however unpleasant he was. This conveyed an image of an idealised mother who was never physically or emotionally absent. Harry's response to Lynn's perceived failure to provide a 'perfect fit' to his needs was a paroxysm of infantile aggression. His anxiety had to be evacuated immediately in retaliatory attacks.

Kohut (1977) observed that some patients relate to their therapists as 'mirrors' or what he called self-objects - an extension of the patient himself rather than an autonomously functioning other. He came to understand that within the narcissistic transference, the therapist functions as a substitute for the patient's missing or defective sense of self. But Mr H realised that he was bound to 'fail' Harry who wanted only soothing empathy from him. For example, his criticism of Harry had only intensified the problem:

> "... the therapist's failure to contain projective identifications can result in ...the patient's re-internalisation of the original projected feelings, combined with the therapist's fears about and inadequate handling of those feelings". (Ogden, 1992a p.33)

At this early stage, Harry could only unconsciously re-enact his separation complex as a form of memory. His difficulties in relationship, and 'need' to experience failure, had arisen straight away in his therapy.

One of Harry's sessions was on a Monday morning. Monday mornings would frequently bring on business 'crises' which would prevent him from attending and members of his exasperated staff would be required to telephone his therapist as well as to find rapid solutions to the business problems.

Harry was arrogantly dismissive of Mr H's attempts to link his current anxiety about the business with his childhood experiences of anxiety or the weekend break in his therapy. He could not grasp the idea of re-imagining his behaviour in terms of an unconscious attempt to communicate. Boundary violations such as cancelled sessions may seem simply to be attacking the therapy, but sometimes they represent the patient's ignorance about intimacy. Hamilton (1982) refers to grasping behaviour as an early example of the infant's capacity to make or break a connection. Narcissus could not grasp the object of his desire; you could say that he did not know what an 'object' is. Patients may say "nothing I do makes any difference ... everything slips through my hand". Grasping is an essential preliminary to object usage (Winnicott, 1971).

Harry's failure to 'grasp' suggested an *avoidant* pattern of insecure attachment. Under these circumstances, it may take a long time to establish the therapeutic alliance. When the alliance is implicit in the attendance of the patient at sessions, during sessions it may seem to be quite absent.

A few months later, Harry began to make critical comments about the consulting-room furniture. He thought it was 'dingy' and 'depressing'. He suggested that it would improve Mr H's 'business image' if he invested in some contemporary chairs and décor. He also found fault with the arrangement of the room. He had read about psychotherapy, and knew how it ought to be. He suggested how the room could be re-arranged.

Mr H felt defensive, for the furniture was his own – and suddenly it *did* seem rather dingy. He made a rather clumsy interpretation linking himself with the loathed stepfather who hadn't looked after Harry properly. Harry enjoyed what he understood as support for his denigration of the stepfather, but dismissed the transference link.

Mostly, the initial negative transference is concealed and denied, but Harry had brought it into the therapy explicitly soon after beginning the work. Technically, it is difficult to establish a working alliance when there is an early negative transference, or negative therapeutic reaction. The patient's unacceptable emotional states combined with ignorance of their meaning, puts him into a painfully humiliating state relative to the therapist. The ensuing feeling of shame is often defended against by grandiose contempt. Harry expressed this both implicitly and explicitly. Disturbing and painful feelings experienced in the counter-transference had made it difficult for Mr H to maintain his therapeutic attitude. He was caught up in a sado-masochistic clinch. After the session, Mr H realised that Harry's contempt was a defence against his own feelings of inadequacy, but within the session he had been caught up in "the numbing feeling of reality" which, Bion said, is indicative of projective identification (Bion, 1961).

Mr H's own narcissistic vulnerability had been touched upon. Winnicott wrote about the many reasons why a mother (or therapist):

> "...hates her infant from the word go'. These include: 'He is ruthless, treats her as scum, an unpaid servant, a slave', and 'He is suspicious, refuses her good food, and makes her doubt

herself, but eats well with his aunt"! (Winnicott, 1947, p. 201)

Before the concept of projective identification had been explored and named, Jung wrote about the 'psychic infections' that can endanger therapists. He described how:

"The patient, by bringing an activated unconscious content to bear upon the doctor, constellates the corresponding unconscious material in him...Doctor and patient thus find themselves in a relationship founded on mutual unconsciousness. It is none too easy for the doctor to make himself aware of this fact." (Jung, 1946, p. 176)

It was as a result of this insight that Jung was the first to recommend the analysis of students of psychoanalysis. Analysis is a precise term in this context, for the purpose is not necessarily (or only) to heal, but to understand in as much detail as possible the elements of the student's psychology, because the psyche is their main tool.

Learning to analyse the transference can be to some extent theoretical, but nothing can prepare one to meet projective identification other than familiarity with one's own infantile object world. The counter-transference that is evoked often first manifests itself in primitive emotions. A positive transference, which subtly flatters the narcissism of the therapist, can be more insidious; at least a negative projection is usually harder to miss!

The following week, Harry described his ideal lifestyle: in a warm country, where pleasures are simple and spontaneous. He contrasted this with Mr H's job, which was perceived as being routine and dull. He spoke scornfully of 'the nine-to-fivers' who needed to 'get a life'. Mr H retaliated by telling Harry that all *he* wanted was to live in a perfect baby-bubble where he could get everything he wanted and needed whilst giving nothing in return. Harry reacted with defensive denial, calling this 'psycho-baby-babble'.

Jung regarded 'symptoms' as purposeful, or teleological, in that they point the way towards where the problem lies. He saw regression, for example, as a patient's attempt to get behind the ordinary defences and into contact with self-images which are usually inaccessible (Jung, 1916, para.146). It is easier to appreciate the value of this from a distance, when hearing a case described by somebody else, for example. It is much harder to hold on to this knowledge when the symptom is enacted within the transference relationship. At its simplest level, the projection of parental images *onto* the therapist generally causes confusion until it is understood. The patient may be reacting *as though* the therapist had been angry and trying to get rid of him. More complex is the situation when projective identification leads to the projection *into* the therapist of unconscious, denied, aspects of the patient. When a patient 'gets inside' through projective identification, there is usually a 'hook' in the therapist's inner world. The patient unconsciously uses these hooks to communicate the "unthought known" (Bollas, 1987). The activation of vulnerable areas in Mr H inevitably led to re-creations of the probable failures in Harry's mother-infant relationship in the transference/counter-transference.

Mr H felt mired in growing feelings of persecuted helplessness. This situation mirrored Harry's sado-masochistic internal object-relation in which aggressive parts of the personality immobilise others by bullying (Steiner, 1993). As long as Mr H was being immobilised by the 'bullying' self, Harry felt relief from his internal persecutor. Although Mr H attempted to meet Harry with empathy, he inevitably sometimes retaliated.

"The necessary facilitating response from the therapist is not usually one which is immediate and spontaneous...the initial spontaneous negative counter-transference feelings...have first to be borne, suitably and not offensively, interpreted, and made bearable to both therapist and patient." (Newton and Redfearn, 1977, p.310)

Mr H. realised that he had not mediated his counter-transference identification, but had just pushed back the painful projection in retaliation, *accusing* Harry, in effect, of *being* a baby. Harry, of course, reacted with defensive denial. The "talion law" (Lambert, 1981), or policy of non-retaliation by the therapist, allows the patient to gradually bear disillusionment about himself, rather than reinforcing the narcissistic barricade. On reflection, Mr H might have been able to contain the splitting and projection by talking about Harry's need to get away from the messy infant feelings that he felt trapped with in psychotherapy.

Mr H felt rather disheartened about his capacity to work with Harry. That night, he dreamt that he was toiling uphill behind Harry, carrying his heavy luggage. On waking, Mr H was shocked to realise how much Harry had 'got inside' him and he took the dream to his own therapy session with some anxiety. His therapist helped him to understand that he had identified with the 'Echo' projection, which met up with aspects of his own internal world. The details of this are not relevant here, but the process is interesting. The personal, unconscious conflicts of the therapist - the 'hook' on which images and projections can hang, 'relates to the indivisibility of the personal and collective factors [in] the area where both the patient and analyst overlap psychologically' (Powell, 1985, p.42). The therapist needs to work on separating his or her own wounds from those of the patient in order to begin thinking symbolically about the material.

Once Mr H had reflected on his disturbing dream, he was able to separate himself from the identification with Harry's projected, disowned, 'baggage'. In supervision, he began to clarify the nature and contents of the baggage: it was heavy, it involved a split between an ignorant, callous Narcissus-self (in front), and a denied burdened Echo-self (behind) - and it was an uphill struggle.

One of the aims of therapy is to try and integrate the 'bad', 'shitty', or 'shadow', aspects of the self. But if the shadow elements are judged immoral by the therapist, the narcissistic defence strengthens, as became evident with the development of Harry's manic defence.

Harry wanted his pain to go away, but 'didn't want to know' about what it represented. Indeed, he bullied the infant self into silence apart from those occasions when it had broken through during the vitriolic fights with Lynn that had brought him into therapy. After a few weeks of therapy, Harry had reacted with an intensification of the split, becoming pre-occupied by grandiose escape fantasies about finding the perfect place or job or partner. Within the narcissistic bubble he appeared unreachable, but when the bubble burst, Mr H realised that what he had been 'carrying' was Harry's unbearable fear of loss.

Negotiating a crisis

Harry telephoned Mr H in a panic late one Sunday night. He said that Lynn had left him because he had been so unreasonable, and the pain in his chest was so acute that he believed he might be about to die. He pleaded with Mr H to tell him what to do, but it was difficult to find the words to reach him. Harry sounded like a terrified, abandoned child, and Mr H found himself speaking very simply, reminding Harry that he needed to have something to eat, and to rest until his session the next morning. Also, with Harry's consent, Mr H made contact with his GP to alert him to the crisis. The GP was helpful, seeing Harry the next morning to check on his physical state, and providing a sick note to give him some time away from work.

Harry came to his session in a desperate state, clinging to Mr H's words as though his life depended on them. Harry's reaction to the loss of Lynn revealed that he had been surviving psychologically only through the presence of a manic defence. When Lynn left him, the archetypal terror broke through. Lynn's departure was, of course, an unbearable repetition of earlier abandonments. Infant feeling-states that have not been sufficiently mediated by benign personal care remain in the psyche with all the overwhelming force of infant experience, but in therapy there is a renewed opportunity to mediate the archetypal state by rendering it meaningful through the transference.

The 'heart-ache' that Harry was experiencing so acutely represented both the breakdown of previous schizoid defences, and an opportunity to learn through suffering. Joseph wrote that such borderline phenomena are:

> "...on the border between mental and physical, between shut-in-ness and emergence, between anxieties felt in terms of fragmentation and persecution and the beginnings of suffering, integration and concern." (Joseph, 1989, p. 89)

Harry's anxiety could not be contained within the established structure of therapy, and he made frequent telephone calls between sessions. Towards the ends of sessions, he would rage that Mr H "sent him away with nothing". Mr H had an image of Harry at this time as a screaming, dirty infant whom he was abandoning at the ends of sessions and weekends in an intolerable state. Harry behaved as though Mr H was withholding the desired supplies deliberately, and "could if he chose" relieve the anguish by 'feeding' him all the time.

The Jungian child analyst, Michael Fordham, wrote about an infant observation during which a little boy was left by his mother. He explained that when as in this case, the "...internalization of the mother image did not take place, the absent real mother leaves her child without her containing and mediating capacities." (1985a, p. 20-21). Fordham noted that "(u)nder these circumstances, the stark archetypal child breaks through in all (its) naked ruthlessness..." (1985a, p.21), and the observer vividly conveyed the boy's catastrophic desperation, describing in detail how his clinging behaviour alternated with violent screaming, yelling, growling, and fierce attacks. Fordham thought that the boy's violent explosions of feeling represented a "total defence of the self" against disintegration. Fordham (1985b) described how absolute, impenetrable defences (e.g. screaming, refusing to listen, flight) come into force against perceived threats to survival. He conceptualised such defences as arising spontaneously from the primary self when the initial mother-infant relationship has failed to transform the overwhelming intensity of archetypal processes.

Whilst Harry experienced himself solely as a helpless infant who could not bear the torrents of feeling and external demands, he used Mr H as an auxiliary ego. This meant that he could accept only empathic interventions, which addressed his infantile emotions. Mr H had to develop a way of talking directly *to* as well as *about* the infant self that was present in sessions. Highly regressed patients become confused when the therapist talks only to the adult in the patient. The infant self has quite a different mode of communication, often through the physiological evacuation of emotion. Remarks addressed to the adult self may be perceived by the infant self as extremely persecuting, and hence misunderstanding is rife. Whilst trying to respond to Harry's rapidly oscillating states, Mr H frequently, of course, 'got it wrong'. When attacks "are expressed in terms of delusion, or through manipulation", (Winnicott, 1971, p.108), they frequently lead to technical 'mistakes' from the therapist.

In the three months after Lynn left, Harry had been very vulnerable with, and dependent on Mr H. One day, Mr H needed to attend a hospital appointment, and so moved all his session times for the appointed day back by half an hour. Unfortunately he forgot to inform Harry of the necessary change, only realising just as Harry arrived for his session. There was twenty minutes left before Mr H had to leave, and on the spur of the moment, Mr H searched his diary and offered a replacement session the next day. Harry accepted, but left saying "you haven't really got the time, have you?" Shortly before Harry was due to attend the replacement session, he telephoned and left a message, sounding distraught, to say that his car had been overheating and he 'couldn't risk' making the journey to therapy. Harry did not come to his next scheduled session either. He wrote to explain that the following week he had to be away 'on business', and ended saying: "Maybe I should send you a month's fees and we'll just call it quits." Mr H telephoned and wrote, but Harry did not return. After a further week, Mr H wrote again, saying that he would hold the session times open for a further month.

Mr H was left to worry about Harry, and think about what had happened. Mr H realised that when he forgot Harry it would have felt as though he had abandoned the baby-self in a ruthless and cruel way. In supervision Mr H's 'forgetting' Harry was explored as an unconscious interaction between the therapeutic couple: Mr H had unconsciously communicated that his need to care for himself came before his commitment to Harry who experienced Mr H as an exploitative and unreliable parent.

He reacted by abruptly abandoning the therapy in a rage. Harry's message about his 'overheating' car represented the boiling over of this narcissistic rage.

The slightest setback suffices to drive a narcissistic patient into a grandiose withdrawal. Rage, resignation and depression precipitate a fall into the "narcissistic hole" (K Asper-Bruggisser, 1987). Often the patient will repeat an infant sado-masochistic clinch by unconsciously manoeuvring the therapist into a position of rejection and the withholding of symbolic narcissistic supplies (Eisenstein, 1951). Shame about dependency may induce a therapeutic stalemate as the patient tries to master his narcissistic injuries (Mollon, 1984). In defence against the pain of being let down, Harry was unconsciously pushed to destroy the therapeutic alliance.

Mr H reflected on the effects of his guilt about forgetting Harry: he had acted out by impulsively offering a replacement session. Mario Jacoby (1985) described how a child may be seduced into relinquishing his own needs in favour of providing support to a needy parent. When caught up in a re-enactment, the therapist similarly can unconsciously 'seduce' the patient into meeting his own narcissistic needs. Mr H's offer to Harry had echoed Harry's narcissistically vulnerable mother, who had sought constant reassurance from him. Within the persecutory atmosphere of the delusional transference, the false note in Mr H's concern had been painfully amplified (Schwartz-Salant, 1982).

An important feature of the Narcissus-Echo meeting is that the potential for a loving connection between the two ends in non-consummation, and in Echo's case a withering of her body, an ossification of her soul. Perhaps the most poignant aspect of the story is its unfulfilled passion: Narcissus had to defend against relationship and eventual separation by adopting a haughty separateness.

Traumatic disillusionments result in *severance* rather than separation, and the rhythmic sequence of *deintegration and reintegration* is broken.

"Within the therapeutic hour, the desire for merger and the violence of separation meet. The initial joy of the long sought for connectedness to the other gives way to longings and anxieties that begin to feel more painful than the suffering the person originally brought to the process. He is faced with the additional task of re-finding those moments of relatedness, experienced perhaps for the first time, between him and the therapist." (Savitz, 1986, p.321-322)

A month later, just as his notice period was about to expire, Harry suddenly telephoned.

He sounded desperately miserable and said he "hadn't got anyone else to talk to". Mr H suggested that he come for his session the next day, which he did. As though there had been no interruption, Harry resumed his complaints about not being helped by therapy. Nevertheless he attended his sessions regularly from then onwards.

When the predominant mode of communication is through projective identification, split-off or unintegrated parts of the patient's internal world are unconsciously projected into the therapist who is forced to deal with them, just as a parent must react to the emotional power of a baby's cries. By leaving his therapy Harry had initially discharged the distressed infant feelings into Mr H, but of course this could not last. The night after his return to therapy, Harry had a dream, only the second he had reported since therapy began.

Ongoing work

In the dream, *Harry saw a bundle of rags and, picking it up, discovered a tiny starving infant, too weak to cry. He quickly put the bundle down again and ran away, hoping no-one would notice and blame him.*

Harry's association to the dream was a memory of having once watched Lynn give patient attention to her baby niece who was crying inconsolably. Harry had felt furious: the baby should have been made to shut up, or left to cry.

In the dream, Harry was frightened of the crying baby and abandoned it ruthlessly, but knew he was doing something wrong. In the associated image Harry had felt tremendous aggression towards the baby. This implied not only a denial of the infant's needs, but also a desire to destroy it. Mr H pointed out the parallel between the dream and what had recently happened between them, suggesting that his own failure in 'forgetting' had been experienced by Harry's infant self not only as an abandonment, but also as the ultimate 'put down'. This meant that Harry had to leave therapy, but his return signalled a memory by the rational Harry of having been helped. Harry considered this interpretation thoughtfully, then said: "I thought you had mucked me around on purpose, to get rid of me, but I suppose you didn't mean it".

Harry's catastrophic suspicion, resulting from Mr H's 'failure', had threatened to destroy the therapy. Harry's dream-infant was in such a hopeless mess that he could not bear it and had to run away – just as he had believed Mr H wanted to do. When too great a narcissistic injury is inflicted on the patient in the therapeutic relationship, it is important to acknowledge our own empathic failure as well as exploring the roots of the patient's susceptibility to such wounding. This mitigates the archetypal splitting and projection processes so that the healing of the wound can be continued (Savitz, 1986). At this point, interpreting only the patient's destructiveness would intensify the splitting.

This sequence of events in Harry's psychotherapy provides an example of the development of "object usage". Winnicott suggested that only when the *subjective object* (phantasy) is destroyed, thereby placing it *outside the area of omnipotent control*, can the *objective object*, which has survived, be *found and used* (Winnicott, 1971, pp.105-107). Such a development depends on the therapist's survival of attacks that can be very difficult to withstand. Harry had unconsciously managed the therapeutic situation so that Mr H had been both 'destroyed', and then 'found' useful. Now, in contrast with the earlier sado-masochistic interactions during which Mr H had been 'carrying his luggage', Harry could share the burden of the therapeutic work.

Harry's dream, his association to it, and his willingness to think about the transference signalled a development of the symbolisation process. During the next few months, Harry was increasingly able to use therapy as a trustworthy container within which meaningful images could arise. Mr H experienced more freedom from identification with the projections into him during sessions and, as the symbolic space opened up, found himself more able to think.

> Harry had been staying with some old friends, who had looked after him like a child. Harry continued to be very distressed, often telling Mr H that he *couldn't* cope. Then one day, annoyed that his friends had asked him to do some shopping, Harry made a 'Freudian slip'. He said "I *won't* cope" rather than "I *can't*". Mr H felt that this was significant: *"can't"* is helpless but *"won't"* is not. He realised that the *"won't"* represented the destructive part of Harry and that a choice was being made, albeit a negative one. Mr H suggested that in *refusing* to cope Harry was punishing Lynn, and himself, for hurting him, but that it was also self-destructive, undermining

Harry's power to grasp at life again. Harry at first denied this, but added that "he supposed he would be ignored again once he was back to normal". Mr H acknowledged Harry's fear of being abandoned if he were to be seen to be capable of managing himself. Harry admitted to suspicions about how kind people were being, knowing that "it couldn't last forever".

This work revealed how Harry got a perverse gratification from the "domination of the narcissistic organisation" (Steiner, 1993). Having become more resilient, Harry could begin to accept his own capacity for emotional bullying. He acknowledged that sometimes he was enjoying his power to *make* his friends look after him. He acknowledged that, perhaps, he was taking advantage of their kindness, and decided that he could move back to his own flat now.

Towards the end of his first year in therapy, Lynn agreed to give their relationship a second chance. One of her conditions was that Harry should accompany her on a 'self-discovery' holiday. This involved various activities such as yoga, meditation, painting and writing, as well as daily group meetings. Harry sent Mr H a picture postcard depicting an ancient vase, saying "this reminds me of the one on your book-shelf". On his return, Harry brought one of his paintings to show Mr H. It depicted *a little man 'about the size of a baby', adrift on a raft in a big ocean. In a corner, 'far away', there was an island on which stood two naked figures: a man and a woman, looking towards the raft.* He told Mr H that during the group discussion that day, he had shown this painting and cried to feel the isolation and vulnerability of the baby-man. He thought that the man and woman on the island represented his parents together and looking at (after) him as they never had been able to in real life.

He cried in the session as he talked about this, and Mr H was also very moved by feelings of sadness. Harry said that he sent the postcard the day afterwards because he was missing Mr H badly. Mr H suggested that the little man on the raft might show how Harry's baby-self had felt adrift, being separated from him. Harry told Mr H that he had felt comforted by imagining coming back to the therapy room.

Mr H went on to suggest that the couple on the island might represent Lynn and himself, holding Harry in mind. Harry agreed, saying that they had both stuck by him, and he felt a warmth that he had never experienced before. Although the baby-Harry was still adrift, and had no way to propel himself towards relationship-island, *he knew that he wanted to be there, and that they were waiting for him.*

Harry remained in therapy for a further two years. There were many ups and downs, but he had become committed to therapy and was increasingly able to work on himself. Harry's haughty defence had only masqueraded as autonomy. Of vital importance in the treatment of his narcissistic disturbance was the careful management of separation, which is the prerequisite for individuation. This can be fostered by the therapist's tolerance of the patient's need for merger and consequent fantasies of omnipotent control but ultimately the patient has to relinquish this 'control' and realise his dependency on the therapist (Ledermann, 1979). Like Narcissus, the realisation of his helplessness brought anguish, but it also gave voice to Harry's 'Echo' and brought a potential for healthy object relating.

People suffering from narcissistic personality disorders require therapeutic treatment that permits the reconstruction within the therapeutic container of the patient's basic narcissistic strivings (Cooper, 1986). Kohut believed that if the therapist does not interfere too much with the patient's regression, allowing expressions of infantile needs for mirroring and idealisation, then progress towards mature relationship occurs naturally. Gordon (1980, p.262) wrote:

"...love invested in the interactions and inter-communications between our various intra-psychic units and entities – rather than identification with any one of them – seems to characterise what Kohut has called the 'transformations of narcissism', and this is surely the hallmark of individuation".

CHAPTER FIVE

The Development of Narcissism as a Clinical Concept

To attempt a comprehensive history of the psychoanalytic concept of narcissism within one chapter would be impossible, for the number of references alone would fill a book. We are therefore restricting ourselves to offering a review of some key thinkers. This is an attempt to simplify a broad field, and in the process we run the danger of over-simplifying. We therefore beg the tolerance of authors mentioned, whose work may be rendered down to a sentence, and of authors whose ideas are omitted for reasons of space.

Freud
In a 1910 essay Freud (1910) raised the possibility of libido becoming attached to objects representing the self. In 'On Narcissism' (1914) he explored this process, opening up the dynamics for further study. He identified an infantile auto-erotic state that is pre-ego: "the libidinal complement to the egoism of the instinct of self-preservation". Freud understood that during early infancy, 'self-love' is natural and necessary, but his clinical investigations led him to distinguish this normal (*primary*) narcissism from pathological (*secondary*) narcissism. Many of the

manifestations of what is today called 'narcissistic disorder' were originally subsumed under Freud's description of secondary or pathological narcissism.

In normal states of crisis, such as bereavement, libido that has already been invested in objects is withdrawn from them. Freud realised that this can also sometimes be observed in pathological states, such as melancholic grief reactions, schizophrenia or sexual perversions. In these situations, too, the normal human movement towards loved objects is arrested. He thought that the loss of a significant love-object in infancy caused defensive withdraw of libido back into the self. The loved object is not only lost, but also hated, because of its association with rejection and profound disappointment. The defences against loss mean that the individual then carried the seeds of pathological narcissism into adulthood, and the capacity for benign attachment to other objects is impaired. Freud's later concepts of the death instinct and the super-ego were built on his understanding of these dynamics (see Green, 2001). In the sense that psychoanalysis explores internal object relations, the entire post-Freudian *oeuvre* has been devoted to the development of Freud's original thoughts about narcissism. Some of the threads of this work are outlined below.

Jung

Freud was developing his concept of narcissism during and immediately after the years of his close association with Jung, between 1906 and 1914. 'On Narcissism' was published just after their irreconcilable break. It refers to controversies with Adler as well as with Jung. It was, to some extent, a rebuttal of Jung's criticism about his definition of libido (see the 'Freud/Jung Letters', McGuire, 1974).

Jung's divergence from Freud's psychoanalytic theory had begun with a disagreement about the exclusively sexual nature of libido (Jung, 1912a). Although this issue had a particularly personal resonance for Jung (see Afterword) he expressed his feelings in terms of theoretical differences. For example, Jung regarded Freud's theory of libidinal withdrawal as an incomplete explanation for the difficulties suffered by schizophrenic patients (see Jung, 1916, paras. 146-7). He observed that his patients' delusions represented different versions of reality that could co-exist. Lacking the more-or-less stable sense of self that mentally-well people take for granted, his patients had many 'selves', or dissociated sub-personalities. From this, Jung evolved his theory of psychological *'complexes'*, each organised around a core conflict, with both personal and archetypal roots. His clinical work focussed on the nature of, and relationships between, these 'selves' (Jung, 1935).

Jung did not write of narcissism as a discrete disorder but developed a different vocabulary for the same phenomena. Narcissism, as such, is only mentioned five times in Jung's writings (Gordon, 1980) but some of his work covered similar ground. For example, he wrote:

> "...to the degree that he does not admit the validity of the other person, he denies the "other" within himself the right to exist – and vice versa. The capacity for inner dialogue is a touchstone for outer objectivity." (Jung, 1916, p. 89)

Jung's notion of mental development rested on the realisation of innate psychological blueprints, which he called *archetypes*. Archetypes are understood as potential patterns in the psyche that represent universal human experiences such as birth, feeding, sexual intimacy and death. During development, these potentials are activated through experiences such as interaction with objects. But when the archetypes are insufficiently mediated during infancy by the primary care-givers, their 'larger-than-life' quality remains. Then, instead of integrated, 'human-sized' objects, the child's psyche remains a prey to overwhelmingly intense primal emotions, which constantly pose a threat to the ego's integrity. An ego so threatened is fragile, or 'narcissistically vulnerable'.

Jung also identified individuals who endure intense suffering, what he called *a passion of the soul*, rather than a disease of the mind (Jung, 1946). He regarded the search for meaning to be the central therapeutic endeavour with these patients. An important aspect of this work is to accept into consciousness those terrifyingly unacceptable (shadow) elements that are reviled and disowned. Working towards maximal awareness of all aspects of the self is a cornerstone of the process of individuation, a lifelong endeavour (see Samuels, Plaut & Shorter, 1986, pp. 76-77). In his paper, 'Jung's Lost Contribution to the Dilemma of Narcissism', Jeffrey Satinover (1984), suggested that Jung's work on *the self* was essentially about what psychoanalysis termed narcissistic development.

Although every person's experience differs, it inevitably contains similar developmental elements. These patterns are fundamental to life across all cultures and each culture expresses these fundamentals in different images. The myth of Narcissus and Echo is an example of such an archetypal image. The story describes one man and one woman, but their interaction can be seen as representative of all individuals, a symbol of intra-psychic processes at a particular point of human development. The archetypal realm can be understood as the 'psychotic-like underlay of the human personality' (Fordham, 1995).

There is, Jung suggested, always a danger of identifying with the 'larger-than-life' archetypal elements in oneself and being 'carried away', or *'possessed'*, by them. In this case, interpersonal relationships are essential to mediating the archetypal elements, to bring them into human proportions. For example, grandiose fantasies of magical omnipotence arising through identification with a heroic archetype can lead someone into reckless acts, though Jung emphasised the capacity of the Self to regulate and take care of the developing individual, even under inauspicious circumstances.

As with most of Freud and Jung's original ideas, later generations of analysts have thoroughly re-worked them in the light of experience. Over the years, the concept of narcissism has become such an integral part of our thinking that it is increasingly difficult to trace developments in it. Almost every text now assumes knowledge of, or includes a reference to, narcissism. One would need a 3D pop-up book to render a picture of the complex weavings of ideas across and within schools.

From a clinical viewpoint, a useful way of conceptualising the different axes of 20th century clinical theory is that of vertical splitting and horizontal splitting. Vertical splitting is the action of dissociation between parts of the self or selves; horizontal splitting is the action of repression from ego to unconscious. The vertical splitting of infancy, which is a natural feature of development, becomes problematic only as a result of traumatic deficiency. To the extent that ego development takes place, the personality then becomes liable to the secondary, horizontal splitting arising from defences such as repression and negation. The splitting in borderline narcissistic states is primarily vertical (Satinover, 1984). Freud, himself, in a short paper (1940), commented on the splitting of the ego as a defence against trauma.

Of course, both directions of split overlap in all of us, to different extents and at different times, and both these models have played an important part in the evolution of approaches to narcissism. Clarification about this differentiation can assist with clinical work as well as with study. Confusions about these views have caused much trouble during the evolution of psychoanalysis. Theoreticians have tended to fall into one of these 'camps': Freud vs. Jung, Klein vs. Kohut and so on. An integrated theory must take account of both, and analysts such as Winnicott, Fordham, and more recently Kalsched (1996), have elaborated their work on this basis. The nature of the psychotherapeutic process is, in either case, to work on the intra-psychic relationship between the split aspects of the patient, through the medium of the transference. In both cases, defensive efforts will be operating, which are designed to prevent the two sides of the split from coming together. Anxiety manifests itself as a signal of threats to these defences.

Klein

Melanie Klein disagreed with Freud's concept of primary narcissism, contending that object relations are present from the beginning of life. She described the mechanisms of splitting and projecting impulses and parts of the self into objects. These processes have a useful defensive function, enabling the infant self to get rid of disturbing feelings, but have the disadvantage of incurring anxiety about the state and intentions of the object. Although Klein herself rarely referred directly to narcissism, she described many aspects of narcissistic functioning as they arise within the paranoid-schizoid position, and these ideas have since been explored and developed in detail.

For example, narcissistic withdrawal has been considered as an omnipotent defence against envy in which the infant's self or body is identified with an idealised object (Sohn, 1985). Paula Heimann (1989) linked this insight with the Narcissus myth. She remarked that on looking into the water, Narcissus saw his reflection as though it were an object, but the reader knows that he was actually looking at himself, or *into* himself. His tragedy was mistaking the unconscious phantasy of a loved object residing within himself, the subject, for an external object.

Although Melanie Klein worked within the Freudian psychoanalytic tradition, some of Jung's ideas resonate with her work. Both postulated the existence of innate mental structures, and Fordham (1995) drew up a table of comparison, the main elements of which are as follows:

Jung	*Klein*
Archetypes	Unconscious phantasies
Importance of the symbol for development of personal and cultural life	Symbols as the basis for the development of the mind
The urge for knowledge and spiritual life	The epistemophilic instinct
The ruthlessness of the unconscious	Paranoid-schizoid position
The two mothers: nurturing and terrible	Good and bad breast mothers
Battle with and triumph over the mother	Manic defence
The uniting symbol	The breast-penis
The *conjunctio*	Primal scene

Kernberg and Kohut

In America, as in Europe, psychoanalysis and analytical psychology developed parallel 'schools'. Jung developed a continuing relationship with America through his own teaching visits and a network of interested students who went to Zurich for training. It was, though, two psychoanalysts, Otto Kernberg and Heinz Kohut, who had a special interest in narcissism. Kohut regarded narcissism as a disorder of the self (Kohut, 1977). His 'self-psychology' can be regarded as having come close to Jung's ideas.

Freud's concept of the ego-ideal included self-esteem regulating functions, which he specifically linked with narcissism (Freud, 1923). Kohut identified an absence of, or defect in, the psychological structure that maintains self-cohesion and self-esteem in certain patients who related to their therapists as 'mirrors', or idealised objects, leading to what he termed 'narcissistic transferences'. In these cases, the therapist functioned as a substitute for the missing or defective self-esteem-regulating psychic structure, or 'self-object', whom the patient would experience and use as extensions of their own self rather than as an autonomously functioning distinct 'other'. Kohut focussed on the effects of maternal deficiency in the aetiology of narcissism and his theory was essentially interactional, rather than intrapsychic. He emphasised the therapeutic value of corrective emotional experience.

His colleague, Otto Kernberg, was somewhat scathing about Kohut's approach, suggesting that his mirroring style avoided confronting the negative transference. Kernberg was interested in the problems of arrogance in his narcissistic patients, understanding that charismatic and successful people can also be despotic and tyrannical. Kernberg made use of Kleinian thinking about unconscious phantasy, emphasising the need for the therapist to confront the negative and destructive elements of the patient's transferences.

Kernberg (1975) regarded Narcissistic Personality Disorder as one type of borderline condition, identifiable by the presence of a grandiose self resulting from defensive splitting into 'mutually unacceptable split ego-states' (Kernberg, 1976a). He described how some patients' 'splendid isolation' functioned as a defence against low self-esteem, envy of the other, and dependency on others. He specifically linked infantile narcissistic difficulties with the failure to successfully resolve later Oedipal conflicts, and hence to difficulties in forming mature sexual attachments in adulthood.

Russell (1985) gave a list of comparisons between Kernberg and Kohut, of which this is a summary. She highlights areas of convergence in their views about pathological narcissism:

1) Patient has a defective self
2) Insufficiently good attachment experiences in infancy
3) Idealised parental images/grandiose self images
4) Psychotherapy centred on grandiose self

...and divergence:

	Kernberg	Kohut
Pathological narcissism	Seen as different from primary narcissism; as a defence against rage and envy	Seen as the same as primary narcissism; as a result of fixation
Aetiology	Late oral stage	Any stage up to latency
Classification	A type of borderline personality disorder	Distinct from BPD
Aggression/ rage seen as	Primary and instinctual; must be confronted in treatment.	Reactive and defensive; should not be confronted in treatment.

Winnicott, Fordham and Bowlby

In the UK after World War II, Winnicott, a psychoanalyst, and Fordham, a Jungian analyst both by chance worked at Paddington Green Children's Hospital, Winnicott as a Consultant Paediatrician, and Fordham as a Child Psychiatrist. Both worked with infants and children, and developed analytic theory from their different standpoints. They have much in common, but with a central difference concerning the mental status of the infant. Winnicott (1960a) regarded the mother-infant unit as primary whereas Fordham (1985c) considered that the infant was born as an integrated self. Both described the primitive defence systems that come into operation when the infant's experience is traumatically disrupted. Whilst the infant's anxieties can be contained within a 'good-enough' holding environment, traumatic failures of holding result in splitting into 'true' and 'false' selves (Winnicott, 1960b) and the fragmentation of the sense of self (Fordham, 1985c). It is the primitive defences of the self that arise in the therapy of narcissistic patients.

Winnicott considered that optimal 'holding' by the environment-mother during infancy was essential for healthy development. He believed that destructiveness had a positive role in the infant's development during self-mother differentiation. Successful 'destruction of the subjective object' (self-object), facilitates the capacity to use an 'objective object' (differentiated other) for 'play' (exploration, learning, relatedness, creativity). He described how certain patients need to

> "...stage the trauma or environmental failure and to experience it within the area of personal omnipotence, and so with a diminished narcissistic wound." (Winnicott, 1989, p.75).

Fordham (1985c) extended Jung's understanding of the individuation process in later life into infancy and childhood. He observed how an infant related to the mother during a feed, nappy-change, play and so on, but at other times withdrew into itself for rumination, digestion and sleep. In his view, the integrated 'primary' self of the infant *'de-integrated'* during relational experiences, and *'re-integrated'* these experiences during quiet times. He contrasted this rhythmic process with occurrences of *dis-integration* when the infant's needs are not met by a sufficiently immediate or appropriate response from the environment. When the powerful, archetypal, experiences of infancy are successfully mediated, the 'larger-than-life' quality of internal objects becomes humanised. Archetypal contents that are not sufficiently mediated remain as objects that repeatedly pose a threat to the ego's integrity. This fragile, narcissistically vulnerable, ego remains liable to fragmentation unless a containing relationship, such as a good marriage or psychotherapy, can take on the task of mediation later in life.

Many therapists and analysts from both the Freudian and Jungian traditions have developed these formulations. Notable 'Winnicottians' include **Christopher Bollas** who has explored the use of the therapist by narcissistic patients as a *transformational object*. Just as the infant must not be asked whether he has 'found' or 'made' his transitional object, so the therapist working in this area must bear with the paradox of being neither and yet both, until the patient can resolve it for himself (Bollas, 1986).

Thomas Ogden developed ideas about the effect of narcissistic wounding on oedipal development in girls: "The transitional relationship with mother mediates the entry into the female Oedipus complex..." (Ogden, 1992b). Successful negotiation of weaning from mother is seen as a model for managing 'otherness'. When the mother allows herself to be a conduit to the other-in-herself, ie. *her own internal father*, the subsequent relationship with external father is not traumatic. But if mother cannot allow herself to be used in this way because of gender insecurities, the little girl will feel narcissistic shame about her femaleness. She may then turn away from father, or seek his love to restore basic feelings of self-esteem, leading in adulthood to an addictive search for men to do the same.

Neville Symington suggested that narcissism is the source of all mental disturbance, saying "...it is a personal problem in all of us which we have to solve..." (1993). He believed that even in early infancy *intentionality* may be observed in a turning away from the breast as a reaction to pain. He regarded this as a *narcissistic choice*, distinguishable from a creative emotional action. Such a choice is an act of spurning what he poetically called *'the Lifegiver'*. 'The

Lifegiver' seems akin to both Winnicott's 'true self', and to the transitional object. Symington cited friendship as an example of a psychological reality that "exists in two people, and yet ... is not entirely contained in them". He considered that the suicide of Narcissus resulted from a glimpse of the terrible tyrant that had smothered his self and prevented it from coming into contact with anything life-enhancing. He cautioned that, similarly, with patients, getting in touch with the 'infantile spontaneous emotional self' often generates despair and brings a risk of suicide.

The 'Developmental' Jungian school in London, founded by Fordham (see Soloman, 1997), has been of importance in bringing together the Classical Jungian approach with insights from psychoanalysis. **Rushi Ledermann** made a major contribution to understanding the disturbances arising from problems during the primary narcissistic phase of development. She considered that these are most likely to arise whilst the infant is beginning to separate from mother and to form a distinct identity. The mother who can tolerate the infant's need for merger contains the omnipotent fantasies until they can gradually give way to the realisation of dependency on her (Ledermann, 1987).

Rosemary Gordon (1980) looked at the place of the mirror in therapy, emphasising the important function of the therapist as a mirror for the patient. **Mario Jacoby**, working from a classical Jungian perspective, also emphasised the significance of the mirror in the Narcissus myth. Narcissists he believed, far from being fixated on their mirror-image, actually perceive themselves in a distorted way that blocks the possibilities of gaining from ordinary experiences of mirroring. He stressed the importance of the therapist respecting these irrational aspects of the patient's world-view. Jacoby also described the dangers at both the individual and collective level when narcissistic rage combines with the search for high ideals and the meaning of life:

"(u)nder these circumstances, rage with all its consequences may flare up 'in the name of' whatever the ideal is (e.g. in the name of Christ, Allah, Mother Church, a perfect society, the Revolution, etc.)" (Jacoby, 1985, p.174)

He said that unacceptable rage is imputed to the shadow, and narcissistic personalities cannot integrate it because self-criticism would mean "I am not perfect – my whole existence is thus absolutely worthless" i.e. "*I am nothing but my shadow*". All attempts to address the shadow directly in therapy are likely to be fraught, causing a 'clash of moralities'.

John Bowlby, a psychoanalyst at the Tavistock Clinic in London, worked on research into children's behaviour during and after separation from mother, analysing images filmed at a residential children's nursery (Robertson & Robertson, 1967-72). He observed that proximity to the mother is essential for development because instinctive attachment behaviours are blocked or immobilised by prolonged separation (Bowlby, 1975). In *de*tachment, signals that would lead to loving and being loved are defensively blocked by selective sensory exclusion. Subsequent research carried out by attachment theorists, such as **Mary Main**, has made an important contribution by identifying three kinds of object-relating associated with disturbed attachment: *avoidant*, *ambivalent* and *disorganised* (see overviews by Marrone, 1998, and Knox, 1999). It is interesting to note that here the focus is on patterns of relationship between internalised representations as, for example, the approach-rejection-withdrawal dynamic of Narcissus and Echo. Problematic attachment patterns can therefore be especially helpful at the stage of assessing a patient for therapy (Main & Goldwyn, 1984).

Bion, Rosenfeld and Steiner

Wilfred Bion took forward the work of Melanie Klein through his work with war victims. He distinguished between two 'personalities' which functioned differently within the same person, calling them 'psychotic' and 'non-psychotic' (1957). Herbert Rosenfeld (1971) elaborated this line of thinking in relation to negative narcissistic organisations in the personality, these often being represented in dreams by the image of a gang.

John Steiner (1993) described how the powerful, destructive, part tyrannises the dependant, needy, part and prevents it from gaining access to good objects. As a way of managing this insoluble conflict, the patient may settle for a stalemate, which Steiner described as a *psychic retreat*. He contrasts this retreat, within which nothing can change, with the potentially creative transitional space of Winnicott. Therapeutic work aims to 'rescue' the infant self from the narcissistic gang. Donald Kalsched, a contemporary American Jungian analyst, has also written about the inner tyrant. He described the evolution of a 'protector-persecutor' sub-personality as a result of trauma. Although this defensive system has the aim of 'self-care', it involves continual attack on the self (Kalsched, 1996).

Sinason (1999) has refined this line of thinking in relation to clinical work. He describes helping a patient to distinguish between her 'mad self', who came within the category of narcissistic character pathology, from her 'usual self' who was frequently taken over by it. Her usual self gradually became able to understand her *'psychotic co-habitee'*, and to regard it with concern and care. Richards (1999) highlighted the clinical implications of this model. Traditionally, the aim of therapy has been to help the patient to understand and reduce splitting, but if the conception is of two psychic structures from birth, with different aims and ways of functioning, the therapeutic aim is to help the patient *differentiate the 'well' from the 'ill' self*. She advocates a 'dual-track' therapy, in which both minds need to be understood and addressed. In this view, therapists also have an 'internal co-habitee', which can be observed in hostile interpretations and so on. Within a session, working out who is disturbed, and why, requires careful and open-minded exploration by both therapist and patient.

Afterword

Jung's antagonism to Freud's 'sexual libido' seems more personal and less theoretical when it is understood that he was in practice unable to maintain a grasp on the erotic transference/counter-transference. Early in his career as a psychoanalyst, Jung became sexually involved with a young patient, Sabina Spielrein. In recent years, this relationship has been extensively studied and written about, notably by Carotenuto (1982). An entire volume of the Journal of Analytical Psychology has been devoted to examining the surviving documentation, including extracts from Spielrein's diary (Spielrein, 1906). Letters exchanged by the lovers show that they were both involved in enacting an incestuous phantasy.

Jung began to correspond with Freud during his affair with Sabina Spielrein, and both participants in it sought his advice and help. Despite knowledge of this affair, for a few years Freud maintained an uneasy alliance with Jung in the interests of developing and promoting the psychoanalytic movement. Their split was inevitable, given the nature of Jung's difficulties with the Oedipal transference. Neither Freud nor Jung had analysts of their own, but with the benefit of hindsight we can consider the possibility that Jung's psychological problems belonged to the pre-Oedipal area of narcissistic borderline pathology.

In his autobiography Jung described his mother as having two personalities: "By day she was a loving mother, but at night she seemed uncanny ...like one of those seers who is at the same time a strange animal...(a)rchaic and ruthless" (Jung, 1963: p. 67-8). When he was still a little boy, his mother was hospitalised for some months, probably with depression. He turned for comfort to a maid who was "...quite different from my mother... It was as though she belonged not to my family but only to me, as though she were connected in some way with other mysterious things I could not understand" (Jung, 1963, p. 23). Jung described how in the following years he "...sensed a splitting..." of himself and evolved two 'personalities', which seem to mirror those ascribed to his mother. One 'personality' was an ordinary schoolboy, but the other was secret, special and mysterious. He carved a little figure to represent it, and kept it hidden in the attic. Knowing that he possessed this 'manikin' gave him an illusion of secret superiority, and helped him to feel powerful in relation to difficulties at home and at school. This boyhood split was the precursor of narcissistic pathology.

Jung's early splitting defence against dependency on an unreliable maternal object was then re-enacted in adulthood. After qualifying as a psychiatrist, Jung married in 1903. The following year he began treating Sabina Spielrein at the Burgholzli Hospital. She recovered enough to begin training as a doctor, but continued to see Jung at his private consulting-room, and the affair began. The atmosphere of narcissistic inflation is unmistakable. Jung characterised Sabina's behaviour as her 'Siegfried complex', meaning her desire to have a special child with him (a reference to the myth of the *Nibelung*, portrayed in Wagner's 'Ring Cycle'). Siegfried was a heroic and tragic figure, and it seems that Jung identified with him. Sabina's interest in Jung's ideas fuelled his grandiosity. Her adoration seems to have gone to his head, and he acted as though he really was a superman, above the law. The unrecognised 'Narcissus-Echo' dynamic then caused Jung to behave quite sadistically towards Sabina who, for her part, masochistically accepted increasing humiliation and rejection.

Given that Jung was such a flawed figure, why is his work worth consideration? When his relationships with both Sabina Spielrein and with Freud ended, Jung descended into internal chaos, which he later called his 'confrontation with the unconscious'. Throughout this period of breakdown, Jung carried out an intense 'self-analysis'. Much of his ensuing work on mythology and primitive ritual, exploring the border between enactment and symbolic thought, was perhaps an attempt to understand this area in himself. Problems arising in this liminal zone, where distinctions between phantasy and reality are unclear, have remained at the heart of psychotherapy. Freud's early dilemma, about whether his patients' reports of childhood sexual experiences with carers were real or imagined, still preoccupies practitioners today.

Although Jung never referred explicitly to his sexual misconduct, his long paper 'The Psychology of the Transference', published in 1946 and dedicated to his wife, represents a milestone in his development. Using the alchemists' *Rosarium Philosophorum* as an allegory, he explored and explained how the archetypal incest complex at work between couples at an unconscious level creates "...the greatest possible confusion". In the same year, 1946, Melanie Klein published 'Notes on some Schizoid Mechanisms', beginning the exploration of projective identification, a concept that renders Jung's experiences more understandable developmentally and hence less mysterious.

Jung's warnings about 'psychic infection', and his emphasis on the necessity for trainee analysts to be analysed themselves, testify to his awareness of the dangers of analytic work. A therapist's own pathology can provide an invaluable tool for understanding patients, provided it has been acknowledged and understood, rather than denied. But even psychotherapists today, with their profound self-knowledge, have no immunity to attacks of 'madness'. In working with borderline states in their patients, psychotherapists are still, like Jung, prone to being taken over by the 'ill self'. Mostly, these take-overs are short-lived, and can be managed within the usual boundaries of the work. Sometimes, and especially when experiencing periods of narcissistic disturbance, the psychotherapist is unable to contain his or her 'ill self' and slips into acting-out behaviour of various kinds. Unfortunately, sexual and financial exploitation of patients does occur and can cause intense suffering. This danger is acknowledged by the training organisations' Codes of Ethics and Practice, which aim to control therapists' behaviour and safeguard patients' interests.

These extremes may seem remote from the everyday practice of most psychotherapists, but ethical issues are not. As Mr H discovered from his dream about carrying Harry's baggage, Narcissus and Echo are never far away.

REFERENCES

Agass, D. (2000). Aspects of narcissism in a once-weekly psychotherapy. *British Journal of Psychotherapy*, 17: 37–50.
American Psychiatric Association: Committee on Nomenclature and Statistics (1994). *Diagnostic and Statistical Manual of Mental Health Disorders (Revised 4th edition)*. Washington DC: American Psychiatric Press.
Asper-Bruggisser, K. (1987). Shadow aspects of narcissistic disorders. *Journal of Analytical Psychology*, 32: 117-137.
Bateman, A. (2000). Integration in psychotherapy: an evolving reality in personality disorder. *British Journal of Psychotherapy*, 17: 147-156.
Berman, J. (1990). *Narcissism and the Novel*. London & USA: New York Univ. Press.
Bion, W. R. (1957). Differentiation of the psychotic from the non-psychotic personalities. *International Journal of Psychoanalysis*, 38: 266- 275. [Also in: *Second Thoughts: Selected Papers on Psychoanalysis: Karnac, 1984*].

Bion, W. R. (1961). *Experiences in Groups*. UK: Tavistock Publications.
Bollas, C. (1986). The transformational object. In: G. Kohon (ed.), *The British School of Psychoanalysis: The Independent Tradition*. London: Free Association Books.
Bollas, C. (1987). *The Shadow of the Object: Psychoanalysis of the Unthought Known*. UK: Free Association Books.
Bollas, C. (1989). *Forces of Destiny: Psychoanalysis and Human Idiom*. London: Free Association Books.
Bowlby, J. (1975). Attachment theory, separation anxiety and mourning. In: S. Arieti (ed.), *American Handbook of Psychiatry (2nd edition)*. USA: Basic Books.
Carotenuto, A. (1982). *A Secret Symmetry: Sabina Spielrein between Jung and Freud*. (Trans. A. Pomerans, J. Shepley and K. Winston). New York: Pantheon.
Carvalho, R. (1982). Paternal deprivation in relation to narcissistic damage. *Journal of Analytical Psychology, 27*: 341-357.
Chodorow, N. (1985). Gender, relation and difference in psychoanalytic perspective. In: C. Zanardi (ed.), *Essential Papers on the Psychology of Women*. USA: New York University Press.
Colman, W. (1998). Contrasexuality and the unknown soul. In: I. Alister and C. Hauke (eds.), *Contemporary Jungian Analysis*. London: Routledge.
Coltart, N. (1988). Diagnosis and assessment of suitability for psychoanalytic psychotherapy. *British Journal of Psychotherapy, 4*: 127-134.
Cooper, A. (1986). Narcissism. In: A. Morrison (ed.), *Essential Papers on Narcissism*. USA: New York University Press.
Dougherty, M. (2001). Love-life: using films in the interpretation of gender within analysis. In: I. Alister and C. Hauke (eds.), *Jung & Film*. UK: Brunner-Routledge.
Eisenstein, V. (1951). Differential psychotherapy of borderline states. *Psychiatric Quarterly 25*: 379-401.

Fordham, M. (1985a). Abandonment in infancy. *Chiron*, 2: 1-23.
Fordham, M. (1985b). Defences of the self. In: *Explorations into the Self*. London & USA: LAP / Academic Press.
Fordham, M. (1985c). Integration – deintegration in infancy. In: *Explorations into the Self*. London & USA: LAP / Academic Press.
Fordham, M. (1995). Freud, Jung and Klein. In: R. Hobdell (ed.), *Freud, Jung, Klein: The Fenceless Field: essays on psychoanalysis and analytical psychology*. London: Routledge.
Freud, S. *The Standard Edition of the Complete Psychological Works of Sigmund Freud (24 Vols.)*; translated by J. Strachey, London: Hogarth Press / Institute of Psycho-Analysis.
Freud, S. (1910). Leonardo da Vinci and a memory of his childhood. *S.E., 11*: 59-137.
Freud, S. (1914). On Narcissism: an Introduction. *S.E., 14*: 67-102.
Freud, S. (1923). The Ego and the Id. *S.E., 19*:1-66.
Freud, S. (1940). Splitting of the Ego in the Process of Defence. *S.E., 23*: 271-278.
Gordon, R. (1980). Narcissism and the self - who am I that I love? *Journal of Analytical Psychology*. 25: 247-263.
Graves, R. (1981). *The Greek Myths*, London: Cassell.
Green, A. (2001). *Life Narcissism, Death Narcissism*. (Trans. A. Weller). London: Free Association Books.
Hamilton, V. (1982). *Narcissus and Oedipus: the Children of Psychoanalysis*, London: Karnac Books.
Hearst, L. (1988). The restoration of the impaired self in group psychoanalytic treatment. In: N. Slavinska-Holy (Ed.), *Borderline and Narcissistic Patients in Therapy*. New York: IUP.
Heimann, P. (1989). Certain functions of introjection and projection in Early Infancy. Chapter note, p.167 in: J. Riviere (ed.), *Developments in Psychoanalysis*. London: Karnac Books.

Hinshelwood, R. (1991). Psychoanalytic formulation in assessment for psychotherapy. *British Journal of Psychotherapy*, 8: 166-174.

Holmes, J. (2000). Attachment theory and psychoanalysis. *British Journal of Psychotherapy,17*: 157-172.

Hopcke, R. H. (1989). *A Guided Tour to the Collected Works of C.G.Jung*. Boston USA: Shambhala.

Jacoby, M. (1985). *Individuation & Narcissism: the Psychology of Self in Jung & Kohut*. USA & London: Routledge.

Joseph, B. (1989). Towards the experiencing of psychic pain. In: M. Feldman and E. B. Spillius (eds.), *Psychic Equilibrium and Psychic Change: Selected papers of Betty Joseph*. London: Routledge.

Jung, C. G. *The Collected Works (20 volumes)*. (Edited by H. Read, M. Fordham & G. Adler, translated by R. F. C. Hull). London: Routledge & Kegan Paul/Princeton University Press.

Jung, C. G. (1912a). The concept of libido. From *Symbols of Transformation, CW vol. 5*: 132-141.

Jung, C. G. (1912b). The battle for deliverance from the mother. From *Symbols of Transformation, CW vol. 5*: 274-305.

Jung, C. G. (1916). The transcendent function. From *The Structure and Dynamics of the Psyche, CW vol. 8*: paras. 131-193.

Jung, C. G. (1934-55). *The Archetypes and the Collective Unconscious, CW9*: 1.

Jung, C. G. (1946). Specific problems of psychotherapy III: the psychology of the transference. From *The Practice of Psychotherapy, CW vol. 16*: 163.

Jung, C. G. (1963). *Memories, Dreams, Reflections*. UK: Collins Fount Paperbacks.

Kalsched, D. (1996). *The Inner World of Trauma: Archetypal Defences of the Personal Spirit*. London and USA: Routledge.

Kernberg, O. (1975). *Borderline Conditions and Pathological Narcissism*. New York: Jason Aronson.

Kernberg, O. (1976a). *Object Relations Theory and Clinical Psycho-Analysis*. New York: Jason Aronson.

Kernberg, O. (1976b). Barriers to falling and remaining in love. In O. Kernberg, *Object Relations Theory and Clinical Psycho-Analysis*. New York: Jason Aronson.

Klein, J. (1999). Assessment – what for, who for? *British Journal of Psychotherapy*, 15: 333-345.

Klein, M. (1975). Notes on some schizoid mechanisms. In: *Envy and Gratitude, and Other Works, 1946-1963*. London: Hogarth Press.

Knox, J. (1999). The relevance of attachment theory to a contemporary Jungian view of the internal world: internal working models, implicit memory and internal objects. *Journal of Analytical Psychology*, 44: 511-530.

Kohut, H. (1977). *The Restoration of the Self*. New York: International Universities Press.

Lambert, K. (1981). *Analysis, Repair and Individuation*. London & New York: Academic Press.

Laplanche, J. & Pontalis, J. (1988). *The Language of Psychoanalysis*. London: Karnac Books.

Lasch, C. (1979). *The Culture of Narcissism: American Life in an Age of Diminishing Expectations*. New York: W.W. Norton & Co.

Ledermann, R. (1987). Narcissistic disorder: a Jungian view of its aetiology and treatment. *British Journal of Psychotherapy*, 3: 359-369.

Ledermann, R. (1979). The infantile roots of narcissistic personality disorders. *Journal of Analytical Psychology*, 24: 107-126.

McDougall, J. (1989). *Theatres of the Body: a psychoanalytic approach to psychosomatic illness*. UK: Free Association Books.

McGuire, W. (Ed.) (1974). *The Freud/Jung Letters, 1906-1914*. UK: Hogarth Press/Routledge & Kegan Paul.

Main, M. & Goldwyn, R. (1984). Predicting rejection of her infant from mother's representation of her own experience: implications for the abused-abusing intergenerational cycle. *Child Abuse and Neglect, 8*: 203-217.

Manzano, J., Palacio Espasa, F. & Zilkha, N. (1999). The narcissistic scenarios of parenthood. *International Journal of Psychoanalysis, 80*: 465-476.

Marrone, M. (1998). *Attachment and Interaction*. UK: Jessica Kingsley Publishers Ltd.

Mollon, P. (1984). Shame in relation to narcissistic disturbance. *British Journal of Medical Psychology, 57*: 207-214.

Neumann, E. (1966). Narcissism, normal self-formation and the primary relation to the mother. *Spring*. New York Analytical Psychology Club.

Newton, K. & Redfearn, J. (1977). The real mother, ego-self relations and personal identity. *Journal of Analytical Psychology, 22*: 295-314.

Ogden, T.H. (1992a). *Projective Identification and Psychotherapeutic Technique*. UK: Maresfield Library.

Ogden, T.H. (1992b). *The Primitive Edge of Experience*. UK: Karnac Books.

Powell, S. (1985). A bridge to understanding: the transcendent function in the analyst. *Journal of Analytical Psychology, 30*: 29-45.

Pulver, S. C. (1986). Narcissism: the term and the concept. In: A. Morrison (Ed.), *Essential Papers on Narcissism*. USA: New York University Press.

Reich, A. (1940). A contribution to the psycho-analysis of extreme submissiveness in women. In C. Zinardi (ed.) (1990) *Essential Papers on the Psychology of Women*, London: New York University Press.

Richards, J. (1999). The concept of internal cohabitation. In: S. Johnson and S. Ruszczynski (Eds.), *Psychoanalytic Psychotherapy in the Independent Tradition*. London: Karnac Books.

Richman, J.A. & Flaherty, J.A. (1990). Gender differences in narcissistic styles. In: E. Plakun (ed.), *New Perspectives on Narcissism*. Washington D.C.: American Psychiatric Press.

Robertson, J. and Robertson, J. (1967-72). *Young Children in Brief Separation* (Film Series). London: Tavistock Centre.

Rosenfeld, H. (1971). A clinical approach to the psychoanalytic theory of the life and death instincts: an investigation into the aggressive aspects of narcissism. *International Journal of Psychoanalysis*, 52: 169-179.

Russell, G.A. (1985). Narcissism and narcissistic personality disorder: a comparison of the theories of Kernberg and Kohut. *British Journal of Medical Psychology*, 58: 137-148.

Samuels, A., Plaut, F. & Shorter, B. (1986). *A Critical Dictionary of Jungian Analysis*. London: Routledge & Kegan Paul.

Satinover, J. (1984). Jung's lost contribution to the dilemma of narcissism. *Journal of the American Psychoanalytical Association*, 34: 401-438.

Savitz, C. (1986). Healing and wounding: the collision of the sacred and the profane in narcissism. *Journal of Analytical Psychology*, 31: 319-340.

Schwartz-Salant, N. (1982). *Narcissism and Character Transformation*. Toronto: Inner City Books.

Siani, R. and Siciliani, O. (2000). Patients with psychosis, psychotherapy and reorganisation of 'the self'; one model of individual therapy: description and pilot study. In: B. Martindale, A. Bateman, M. Crowe & F. Margison (Eds.), *Psychosis: Psychological Treatments and their Effectiveness*. London: Gaskell.

Sinason, M. (1999). How can you keep your hair on? In: P.Williams (Ed.), *Psychosis (Madness)*. London: Institute of Psychoanalysis.

Sohn, L. (1985). Narcissistic organisation, projective identification, and the formation of the identificate. In: E. B. Spillius (Ed.), *Melanie Klein Today Vol. 1: Mainly Theory*. London: Routledge.

Soloman, H. M. (1997). The developmental school. In: P. Young-Eisendrath and T. Dawson (Eds.), *The Cambridge Companion to Jung*. UK: Cambridge University Press.

Spielrein, S. (1906/7). Unedited extracts from a diary. In: *Journal of Analytical Psychology*, 46: 155-173.

Steiner, J. (1993). *Psychic Retreats: Pathological Organisations in Psychotic, Neurotic and Borderline Patients*. London: Routledge.

Stolorow, R. D. (1986). Towards a functional definition of narcissism. In: A. Morrison (Ed.), *Essential Papers on Narcissism*. USA: New York University Press.

Symington, N. (1993). *Narcissism – a New Theory*. London: Karnac Books.

Wharton, B. (1990). The hidden face of shame: the shadow, shame and separation. *Journal of Analytical Psychology*, 35: 279-300.

White, J., Berry, D., Dalton, J., Napthine, G., Prendeville, B. & Roberts, J. (2001). Holding and treating severe disturbance in the NHS: the containment of borderline personality disorders in a therapeutic environment. *British Journal of Psychotherapy*, 18: 89-105.

Winnicott, D. W. (1947). Hate in the countertransference. In: *Through paediatrics to Psycho-Analysis*. UK: Hogarth Press.

Winnicott, D. W. (1960a). The theory of the parent-infant relationship. In: *Maturational Processes and the Facilitating Environment*. London: Hogarth Press.

Winnicott, D. W. (1960b). Ego distortion in the true and false self. In: *Maturational Processes and the Facilitating Environment*. London: Hogarth Press.

Winnicott, D. W. (1971). The use of an object and relating through identification. In: *Playing and Reality*. London: Penguin.

Winnicott, D. W. (1989). Further remarks on the theory of the parent-infant relationship. In: C. Winnicott, R. Shepherd & M. Davis (Eds.), *Psycho-Analytic Explorations by D.W.Winnicott*. UK: Karnac Books.

INDEX

Agass, D., 40, 85
American Beauty (film), 2
American Psychiatric Association, 38, 85
Anna Karenina, 2
archetypes, 10, 24, 69, 73
arrogance/arrogant attitude, 33, 40, 74
Asper-Bruggisser, K., 33, 60, 85
attachment theory, 46, 51, 68, 79

Bateman, A., 40, 85
Berman, J., 2, 85
Berry, D., 40, 92
Bion, W. R., 52, 80, 85–86
Bollas, C., 26, 54, 77, 86
Bowlby, J., 75, 79, 86

Carotenuto, A., 81, 86
Carvalho, R., 48, 86
Chodorow, N., 11, 86
Colman, W., 11, 86
Coltart, N., 35, 86

Cooper, A., 65, 86

Dalton, J., 40, 92
defence(s), 52, 58, 71–73, 75–76, 82
  against loss, 48, 68
  manic, 56–57, 73
  narcissistic, 16, 29, 33, 56
  of the self, 58, 76
  omnipotent, 26, 69
  paranoid–schizoid, 6
  pathological, 7
  psychic retreat, 80
  repression and negation, 71
  schizoid, 57
  with the aim of self-care, 80
definitions, 31, 68
Diagnostic and Statistical Manual of Mental Disorders (DSM-IV), 38–39
Dougherty, M., 2, 86

Eisenstein, V., 60, 86

Flaherty, J. A., 35, 91

Fordham, M., 58, 70–72, 75–76, 78, 87
Freud, S., 1, 3, 67–69, 71–73, 81–83, 87

gender issues, 10–12, 29, 34–35, 77
Goldwyn, R., 79, 90
Gordon, R., 66, 69, 78, 87
grandiosity/grandiose self/fantasies/affectations, 19, 33–34, 39–40, 52, 56, 60, 70, 74–75, 82
Graves, R., 5, 87
Green, A., 68, 87

Hamilton, V., 9–10, 51, 87
Hearst, L., 41, 87
Heimann, P., 72, 87
Hinshelwood, R., 35, 88
Holmes, J., 46, 88
Hopcke, R. H., 11, 88
How to Marry a Millionaire (film), 2
humiliation, 9, 19, 27, 36, 82

idealisation/idealised, 7, 34, 36, 38, 43, 50, 66, 72, 74–75
identification, 7, 10, 12, 34–35, 48, 56, 61, 63, 66, 70
  adhesive, 7
  with the aggressor, 24
  projective, 36, 50, 52–54, 61, 83
    and 'psychic infection', 53, 83
    'hook' in the therapist, 54–55
    counter-transference, 54–55
individuation, 14, 25, 47, 65–66, 70, 76

Jacoby, M., 60, 78–79, 88
Joseph, B., 57, 88
Jung, C. G., 3, 10–11, 14–15, 21, 53–54, 68–73, 76, 81–83, 88

Kalsched, D., 47, 71, 80, 88
Kernberg, O., 32, 34, 73–75, 88–89
Klein, J., 35, 89
Klein, M., 71–73, 80, 83, 89

Knox, J., 79, 89
Kohut, H., 50, 65–66, 71, 73–75, 89

Lambert, K., 55, 89
Lasch, C., 2, 89
Ledermann, R., 62, 65, 78, 89

Main, M., 79, 90
Manzano, J., 19, 90
Marrone, M., 79, 90
McDougall, J., 46, 89
McGuire, W., 68, 89
mirrors/mirroring, 8–9, 16, 19, 28, 36, 50, 54, 66, 74, 78, 82
Mollon, P., 60, 90

Napthine, G., 40, 92
Neumann, E., 24, 90
Newton, K., 55, 90

Oedipal issues, 10, 16, 19, 74, 77, 81
Ogden, T. H., 50, 77, 90
omnipotence/omnipotent, 8, 26, 35, 63, 65, 70, 72, 76, 78
Othello, 43

Palacio Espasa, F., 19, 90
Persona (film), 2
personality disorder(s), 3, 38–40, 47, 65, 74–75
Plaut, F., 70, 91
Portrait of a Lady, 2
Powell, S., 55, 90
Prendeville, B., 40, 92
psychosis/psychotic, 18, 24, 31, 38, 70, 80
  'psychotic co-habitee', 80
psychosomatic symptoms, 35–36, 46
Pulver, S. C., 1, 90

Redfearn, J., 55, 90
Reich, A., 34–35, 90
research findings, 3, 40, 79
Richards, J., 80, 90
Richman, J. A., 35, 91
Roberts, J., 40, 92

Robertson, J., 79, 91
Rosenfeld, H., 80, 91
Russell, G. A., 74, 91

sado-masochism, 29, 32, 33, 54, 63
  and Echo's plight, 9
  and grudge, 21
  and Jung and Spielrein, 82
  dynamic, 35
  sado-masochistic clinch, 52, 60
  sexual, 32
Samuels, A., 70, 91
Satinover, J., 70–71, 91
Savitz, C., 61, 63, 91
Schwartz-Salant, N., 60, 91
separation, 8, 14, 17, 25, 48, 50, 60–61, 65
  and disillusionment, 29
  and heroic task, 15, 37
  and individuation, 25, 65
  and merger/re-merger, 7
  and mourning, 48
  and pseudo-independence, 7
  as opposed to severance, 60
  from mother, 15, 20, 79
  traumatic, 21
Shorter, B., 70, 91
Siani, R., 40, 91
Siciliani, O., 40, 91
Sinason, M., 80, 91
Sohn, L., 72, 91

Soloman, H. M., 78, 92
Spielrein, S., 81–82, 92
splitting, 2, 19, 24, 40, 55, 60, 71, 74, 80
  archetypal, 7, 62–63
  dangers of, 40
  in Klein, 72
  Jung's two 'selves', 82
  Narcissus–Echo, 7
  paranoid–schizoid, 7
  'true' and 'false' selves, 76
  vertical–horizontal, 71
  victim–perpetrator, 30
Steiner, J., 54, 64, 80, 92
Stolorow, R. D., 31–32, 92
suicide, 26, 43, 47, 78
Symington, N., 40, 77–78, 92

transference/counter-transference, 54
  communication, 47
  erotic, 81
  negative therapeutic reaction, 52, 55
  re-enactment, 14

Wharton, B., 36, 92
White, J., 38, 92
Winnicott, D. W., 51–53, 59, 63, 71, 75–76, 78, 80, 92

Zilkha, N., 19, 90